Dear Fellow Member:

I am happy to send you this special limited edition of *Since You Asked* by Paul R. Van Gorder. Please accept it as my way of saying, "Thank You" for your prayerful support of Radio Bible Class.

This book is a compilation of the answers to Bible questions Paul Van Gorder has written for the *Newsletter* and *RBC Discovery Digest.* He discusses a wide variety of Scripture passages and topics that have often troubled serious students of God's Word. I'm sure you'll find the answers to many of your questions about the Bible within these pages.

So again, thank you. And may God bless you richly "with all spiritual blessings" (Ephesians 1:3).

Teacher, Radio Bible Class

Since You Asked...

Bible Questions Answered By

Paul R. Van Gorder

HOW TO USE THIS BOOK

A compilation such as this, containing answers to questions in Bible passages and topics, is most valuable when the subjects or verses can be readily found. For that reason we have provided a complete double index—one for topics and another for Scriptures. If you therefore are looking for a particular passage from Genesis 3:15 to Revelation 20:12, you will find the page number indicated in the back of the book. Or, if you wonder about a specific topic (for example, the shekinah, death, or baptism), you will find it in the subject index. Questions on similar topics have been grouped together for easy comparison.

INTRODUCTION

One of the most rewarding dividends of a Bible-teaching ministry is the warm response of God's people. Especially encouraging to me has been the personal interest in the Bible, indicated by questions from our readers and listeners. Many of these inquiries have been answered by letter. Some have found their way into the pages of the Radio Bible Class *Newsletter* in a column called, "From the Teacher's Notebook." In more recent years, these questions and answers have appeared in the *RBC Discovery Digest* on the page entitled, "Since You Asked."

Some months ago, Leona Hertel suggested that these be compiled for publication in book form. Consequently, most of the work of preparing this manuscript for printing has been done by her. No novice in this work, she compiled, arranged, and indexed the material written by our beloved founder Dr. M. R. De Haan to be used in his question and answer books. To Leona and the RBC Editorial Staff, therefore, I am most grateful. How blessed to have such co-laborers!

May our Lord be pleased to use this book to whet your spiritual appetite for a more diligent study of His Word. And as you do this, the commendation of those believers at Berea will be yours also: " ... they received the Word with all readiness of mind, and searched the Scriptures daily, whether those things were so" (Acts 17:11).

Paul R. Van Gorder

ADAM AND EVE

1. Were Adam and Eve saved? Was it Adam who taught Abel to love God, or did the Lord reveal Himself to Abel in some special way?

Adam and Eve undoubtedly repented and received forgiveness, for God taught them the truth of salvation when He clothed them with skins from a slain animal. They learned that their own righteousness, symbolized by their fig-leaf covering, could never bring release from sin's penalty, and that "without shedding of blood is no remission." The death of the animals and the covering of skins for the fallen pair is a beautiful picture of the sacrifice that Christ, the Lamb of God, made on the cross of Calvary.

As far as Abel is concerned, we have no doubt that he learned the way of salvation from his parents. They must have told him about their sin and God's provision through a blood sacrifice. Romans 10:17 says that "faith cometh by hearing," and it is obvious that Abel believed, for he brought by faith the sacrifice which involved the shedding of blood. Hebrews 11:4 says of Abel, ". . . he obtained witness that he was righteous, God testifying of His gifts . . . ." We therefore conclude that he heard the truth through the witness of his parents, but that God showed Abel in some special way that his offering was accepted.

APOSTASY

2. Please tell me what an apostate is. I have heard certain religious men referred to as "apostates."

An apostate is a person who once professed to believe the truth but then turned from it. Notice the words, "professed to believe." These men knew revealed truth, yet deliberately rejected it.

The apostle John spoke of them as follows: "They went out from us, but they were not of us" (1 John 2:19). Read the entire verse and you will see that apostates are never born-again persons. We get into difficulty whenever we try to determine the genuine from the false. Make sure of this—no apostate has ever had eternal life abiding in him.

Apostasy and backsliding are not the same. Judas is an example of an apostate—though he knew the truth well and witnessed Christ's miracles, he was never saved. Peter, however, was a backslider—a saved man whose fellowship with the Lord was broken by denial, but who was restored.

A helpful footnote on "apostasy" appears in the *New Scofield Reference Edition* of the Bible at 2 Timothy 3:1.

BAPTISM

3. I have been reading Romans 6 and I'm confused about verses 3 and 4. Do they teach believer's baptism, or are they saying that all believers are baptized as an act of Christ apart from immersion?

Know ye not that, as many of us as were baptized into Jesus Christ were baptized into His death?

Therefore, we are buried with Him by baptism into death, that as Christ was raised up from the dead by the glory of the Father, even so we also should walk in newness of life (Romans 6:3,4).

In the days of the apostles there was no such thing as an unbaptized believer. The apostles were faithful to the Lord's command to make disciples, to baptize them, and to observe the things He had commanded. Shortly after a person was saved, therefore, he was encouraged to participate in this ordinance.

Verse 3 reads, "as many of us as were baptized. . . ," which seems to suggest that some were not. The phrase would be more accurately rendered, "all we who were baptized," indicating that the apostle was referring to all believers of the early church without exception.

The passage speaks of immersion into and emergence from the baptismal water as a symbol of our death, burial, and resurrection with Christ. This act is the believer's confession to the world of his identification with Christ in these three aspects of salvation.

Verses 5 through 7 make it clear that every Christian, in God's reckoning, has been crucified with the Lord Jesus and raised with Him. This spiritual experience, which takes place when a believer is justified through faith, is to be followed by the act of baptism in water. The apostle was referring to this when he wrote, "Therefore, we are buried with Him by baptism into death."

4. Please explain what Paul meant when he spoke of being "baptized for the dead" (1 Corinthians 15:29).

As in every Scripture, the safest procedure is to consider the context. In verse 12 of this chapter, the apostle began a sevenfold argument for the resurrection of the dead, climaxing with the exultant declaration, "But now is Christ risen from the dead. . ." (v. 20). Then follows a parenthesis until you reach verse 29. Here the apostle returns to the thought of verse 19. Study this connection.

Verse 29 has been used by a cult as the basis for belief in a vicarious baptism, in which a living friend receives the rite as proxy for a person who died without it. This is really a form of baptismal regeneration, which is not taught anywhere in the Bible. This practice amounts to a pagan ceremony, because salvation is "by grace through faith" alone.

You will note that the apostle was speaking of the physical hazards he and other Christians endured because of their witness for Christ (vv. 30,32). He pictured the Christian life as one of trail, suffering, persecution, and even physical death. Some believers endured death because of their testimony. Then Paul mentioned others "who are being baptized IN PLACE OF those who have died. . . ." The preposition *uper* is translated in the *Authorized Version* as "for." It may just as well be translated "in place of, over, or on the part of." They were not being baptized for the benefit of the dead—*not at all.* Rather, as those who were now stepping into the ranks of the Christian church, they were "in place of" those who had died.

Paul argues, "Why recruit others to replace the dead, if we are fighting a losing battle, and if the dead rise not?" If there is no resurrection it would be pointless to replace martyred saints with other believers who may face the same death.

Baptism is the uniform of the soldier. Early Christians were baptized as a public testimony to their identification with Jesus Christ. For some, it meant putting themselves in the place of possible martyrdom. As some laid down their lives for Christ, others took their place and were "baptized in place of the dead." Reginald Heber wrote, "A noble army, men and boys, the matron and the maid,/ Around the Savior's throne rejoice, in robes of light arrayed./ They climbed the steep ascent of heaven through peril, toil, and pain:/ O God, to us may grace be given to follow in their train!"

5. **Please explain the meaning of John the Baptist's words, "He shall baptize you with the Holy Spirit, and with fire" (Matthew 3:11). Was this the fire experienced on the day of Pentecost?**

Some Bible scholars teach that the baptism of fire did take place at Pentecost, and they use this statement of John the Baptist as the basis for their belief. But I disagree. In this incident multitudes were being baptized in the Jordan, but many Pharisees were present who ignored this baptism (see Matthew 3:5-12). Actually, John the Baptist was addressing two classes of people—the repentant and those who refused to confess their sins—when he said, "He shall baptize you with the Holy Spirit, and with fire."

You will note that in John 1:33 and again in Acts 1:5, no mention is made of the baptism with fire. In the Acts passage, the Lord Jesus was speaking to His disciples, commanding them to wait "for the promise of the Father." Referring to the fulfillment of that promise, He said, "Ye shall be baptized with the Holy Spirit." But the Lord Jesus said nothing about a "baptism with fire." The reason He did not include this in His instruction to the disciples is that believers do not go through it.

Verse 12 of Matthew 3 clearly indicates that our Lord was dealing with two separate classes of people. John said Christ will "gather His wheat into the granary, but He will burn up the chaff with unquenchable fire." Two groups are identified: the *wheat* and the *chaff.* I believe the baptism with the Holy Spirit and the baptism with fire must be for these two different groups respectively. No believer will experience the "baptism with fire"; nor did this baptism take place at Pentecost. We must be careful to observe what Luke's account says and what it does not say. In Acts 2:3 we read, "There appeared unto them tongues as of fire," not "tongues of fire."

The "baptism with fire" is future. Some verses to study in this connection are Malachi 4:1; Mark 9:46-49; Luke 3:17; 2 Thessalonians 1:8. "Fire" in Matthew 3:12 is therefore not figurative of blessing, but of the very opposite.

Believers have received the baptism of the Holy Spirit. *All* who have been born again have experienced it. "For by [in] one Spirit were we all baptized into one body, whether we be Jews or Greeks, whether we be bond or free; and have been all made to drink into one Spirit" (1 Corinthians 12:13). This baptism with the Spirit makes us members of the body of Christ, as the context of 1 Corinthians 12 clearly indicates. The New Testament contains no command for believers to seek the baptism *with* or *in* the Holy Spirit, because it was by this baptism that they were placed into the church which is His body. It is a historical fact in the experience of every believer.

No child of God will ever experience the "baptism with fire," when God will "burn the chaff" in judgment. The warning of Matthew 3:7-11 confirms the interpretation that the "baptism with fire" is the same as the burning up with "unquenchable fire" in Matthew 3:12.

6. Is the baptism which John commanded the same as Christian baptism?

No, it is not. John's baptism was "unto repentance." You will recall that the disciples of John, mentioned in Acts 19, were baptized again. This event followed the death and resurrection of Jesus Christ. When our Lord was baptized by John in the Jordan River, He was simply showing what He had come to do—to take the sinner's place in death. It is wrong to equate Christian baptism with the baptism John administered to the multitude that came out into the wilderness. To do this is to confuse the message of the kingdom to Israel with the good news of salvation through faith in Christ's finished work. While the "baptism of John" spoke of repentance, Christian baptism portrays the believer's identification with Christ in His death, burial, and resurrection.

7. Does Mark 16:16 teach that one must be baptized in order to receive salvation?

No, it does not! The second clause of the verse makes this quite clear, for it declares, "... he that believeth not shall be damned," and no mention of baptism is made. If baptism were essential to salvation, it would have been included in such key passages as John 3:16, Acts 16:31, Ephesians 2:8,9, and Romans 10:9,10. We must never form a doctrine on one isolated phrase of one verse of the Bible when numerous other Scripture references state the doctrine clearly.

8. Please explain Acts 22:16, "Arise, and be baptized, and wash away thy sins, calling on the name of the Lord." Were Paul's sins removed by being baptized?

This verse does *not* teach that Paul was to be cleansed of his sins through his being baptized. He was commanded to do three things: (1) arise, (2) be baptized, and (3) have his sins washed away. The verbs are all imperatives. They are followed by the participle "calling," which may modify all three verbs and may mean that Paul called on the name of the Lord simultaneously with his rising, being baptized, and having his sins washed away. But this doesn't make good sense, and therefore it seems best to take the participial phrase as instrumental in usage. (Other examples of this construction occur in Matthew 6:27, Acts 16:16, and 1 Timothy 1:12.) The text would then read, "Rise up, be baptized, and wash away your sins by calling on the name of the Lord." It was the calling on the Lord's name, not the rising up or the being baptized that brought forgiveness.

BEAST

9.   Who are the "great harlot" and "beast" of Revelation 17? Why is the word "Babylon" written on her forehead?

The "harlot that sitteth upon many waters" (v. 1) is Babylon in its ecclesiastical form. The "many waters" represent the nations over which this false religion will rule (vv. 1,15). In both the book of Revelation and in Old Testament prophecy, Babylon has a larger meaning than simply the ancient city. It is a powerful anti-God *system* that had its origin in Babel and the revolt of Nimrod and which will continue to the endtime. This way of life has both a religious and a political manifestation. The "harlot" is *ecclesiastical* Babylon, including apostate Christendom and possibly all religions that directly oppose Christ and the true church. The "beast" upon which she rides is *political* Babylon, the last form of Gentile world dominion. According to John's prophecy, ecclesiastical Babylon will be destroyed by political Babylon (Revelation 17:16), which in turn will meet its doom at the coming of the Lord Jesus Christ in power and glory.

10.   Is Judas the seed of the serpent mentioned in Genesis 3:15? Could he be the beast of Revelation 17:8?

We have no scriptural authority for accepting either of these suggestions. Presumably, the seed of the serpent is

Antichrist, for Satan is always imitating and counterfeiting the true. His masterpiece of deception will be the "man of sin." Since the expression "the son of perdition" is found both in John 17:12 referring to Judas and in 2 Thessalonians 2:3 indicating Antichrist, some believe that Judas will be reincarnated or resurrected as the beast of Revelation 17:8. Admittedly, this is possible. We dare not be dogmatic, however, about that which Scripture does not speak with certainty.

11. **Who gave power to the second beast of Revelation 13:15, which says that he should "give life unto the image of the beast, that the image of the beast should . . . speak . . . "?**

I believe that the source of the second beast's power is the same as that of the first beast, which had arisen out of the sea. We're told that ". . . they worshiped the dragon who gave power unto the beast" (Revelation 13:4). Therefore, Satan gave the first beast his power and authority. Verse 12 of this chapter tells us that the second beast, the one that came up out of the earth "exerciseth all the power of the first beast before him." The literal translation of these words is, "He exerts all the authority of the first beast in his presence." They both derived their power from the same source—Satan.

BIBLE

12. **Do New Testament Christians have the right to appropriate for themselves the promises of the Old Testament? I'm thinking about such statements as these: "Thou wilt keep him in perfect peace, whose mind is stayed on Thee, because he trusteth in Thee" (Isaiah 26:3). "Fear thou not; for I am with thee. Be not dismayed, for I am thy God" (Isaiah 41:10). "For I, the Lord Thy God, will hold thy right hand, saying unto thee, Fear not, I will help thee" (Isaiah 41:13). "Call unto Me, and I will**

answer thee . . . " (Jeremiah 33:3). These are precious promises.

Every portion of Scripture has a *primary interpretation,* and we do well to look for it first. We must always interpret the Word of God according to its context. This will point us to the basic meaning of a particular passage.

Although there is one primary interpretation of a passage, there may be many *applications.* Christians today do have scriptural warrant for claiming by application the truths of the Old Testament like those listed above. Paul wrote, "Now all these things happened unto them [Israel] for examples, and they are written for our admonition, upon whom the ends of the ages are come" (1 Corinthians 10:11).

In addition, the great principles of Scripture about the faithfulness, love, care, and protection of God for His own do not change. This is because God Himself is immutable. He is truly the same yesterday, today, and forever. Because this is true, the promises of the Old Testament that stem from His character do not change.

The promises you mentioned from the Old Testament, even though spoken to Israel, have exact counterparts in the New Testament. Remember, all Scripture is not written *to* us, but all Scripture is written *for* us.

To assume that the blessed promises of the Old Testament are not for us is an error. Many of them are centered in God's unchangeable character and apply to us as well. No one would deny, for example, that Christians today can still trust in the statement, "The Lord is my Shepherd; I shall not want" (Psalm 23:1). In fact, I would urge a renewed study of the Old Testament. What you find there will be comforting, challenging, and refreshing.

13. Why was there so much stigma about a dead body in the Old Testament?

The regulations concerning the bodies of the dead are found in Numbers 19:11-22. They were given by Jehovah specifically for Israel. Two primary reasons are involved: (1) a quarantine was imposed for purposes of health and the prevention of disease; (2) a dead body symbolized for God's people the full gravity and ultimate consequences of sin. They looked upon death as unnatural. By contrast, the pagans saw it as something intended by nature. The heathen were therefore afraid of death, but they did not abhor it as the Israelites, who saw it as the penalty for sin. By treating a dead body as ceremonially unclean, the Lord's people expressed the fact that death in itself is contrary to the nature of man as the image-bearer of God. It is an anomaly he must endure because of his sin.

14.   After rising from death, Christ ate fish and bread. Will we need food in our resurrection body?

This incident does not indicate that the believer's glorified body will require food. We're told that the Lord Jesus ate "broiled fish, and an honeycomb" (Luke 24:42). The context suggests that He did this to prove to His disciples that He was not a spirit, but that He had a body with "flesh and bones." It was an authentication of His bodily resurrection (see Luke 24:36-43).

"BOOKS" OF REVELATION

15.   Would you please explain the books mentioned in Revelation 20:12? What are these books, and how many will there be?

John saw "books" being opened. Only one of these books is named—the "book of life." The remainder contain the record of the works of those to be judged. The people who are standing before the great white throne are the wicked dead. These books will present ample proof that they are guilty before God. It also seems that what is written in them will determine the degree of their punishment. The penalty will be commensurate with the person's guilt. The life of each unbeliever is brought into review at this judgment, and the "book of life" will be a further record against them. When opened, that book will not contain his name, and he will be denied entrance to Heaven.

CAIN

16. What was the "mark" God placed on Cain after the killing of Abel? (Genesis 4:15).

I believe this represented a pledge God made to Cain. The *American Standard Version* of 1901 translates Genesis 4:15, "And Jehovah appointed a sign for Cain . . . ." The word translated "mark" or "sign" is the same term used in Genesis 9:12,13, "This is the *token* of the covenant . . . ." God promised Noah and his family that He would not again destroy all flesh with a flood, and He gave them the sign of the rainbow to verify it.

We do not know what physical mark God gave Cain to single him out. And, where Scripture is silent, we must not presume to speak.

CHRIST

17. How do your reconcile the words of Jesus in John 3:13 with the fact that Elijah went up by a whirlwind into Heaven?

We must note carefully what Christ did *not* say here. He did *not* say that no man has *entered* Heaven. Rather, He said, "No man hath *ascended* to heaven." The Greek word translated "ascended" in this verse is *anabaino,* and it means "to go up, to climb, to spring up, to ascend." The idea expressed by this word is that of "going up" by one's own power rather than being "taken up." Arthur Pink calls attention to this, pointing out that it is but another example of the marvelous accuracy of Scripture. Enoch was "translated." Elijah "went up by a whirlwind." The saints shall be "caught up." But Christ "ascended." All others who go into Heaven are dependent upon a power outside of themselves. The Lord Jesus Christ "ascended" into Heaven in His own right and by His own power.

18. What is the meaning of Hebrews 9:11,12? Am I to understand that Christ actually entered Heaven with His own blood?

Equally sincere students of the Bible have disagreed on the interpretation of this passage. It reads,

> But Christ being come an high priest of good things to come, by a greater and more perfect tabernacle, not made with hands, that is to say, not of this building,
> Neither by the blood of goats and calves, but by His own blood He entered in once into the holy place, having obtained eternal redemption for us (Hebrews 9:11,12).

I personally do not believe that Christ went into Heaven with His blood. Note that verse 12 does not say He entered Heaven *with* His own blood, but *by* (or through) His own blood. The Greek preposition *dia* may be translated "through," "by reason of," or "by virtue of." Christ is now seated in Heaven as high priest *by virtue of* His glorified humanity, and *by virtue of* His sacrificial death.

The idea of carrying actual blood into Heaven is not justified by the passage. Remember, this "more perfect tabernacle" in Heaven was "made without hands." The context, therefore, does not allow for the admission of any literal material of earth. Besides, Christ's blood was efficacious the moment it was shed, as was evidenced by the torn veil in the temple.

19. In John 20:17 our Lord said to Mary, "Touch Me not; for I am not yet ascended to My Father." In the Scofield Bible, a note mentions Christ as taking His blood to Heaven. Is this mentioned anywhere in the Bible?

The *Scofield Reference Edition* of the Bible gives three views on the interpretation of this passage. I personally hold that our Lord was intent on fulfilling the type given in Leviticus 23:10,11, the feast of firstfruits. On this first day of the week, perhaps at the very time He was appearing to Mary, the high priest in Israel was waving two sheaves of newly cut grain in the temple. This was the harbinger of the harvest to follow. First Corinthians 15:23 indicates the order: "Christ the firstfruits." In fulfillment of the Old Testament feast, Christ presented Himself before the Father. The full harvest, the resurrection of the saints, would occur later. A short time after this, the Lord invited His disciples to "handle and see." He was indicating that the work He had in mind when He said to Mary, "But go to My brethren, and say unto them, I ascend unto My Father," was finished.

20.   What did our Lord mean when He spoke these words from the cross, "My God, My God, why hast Thou forsaken Me?" (Matthew 27:46).

This cry from the cross was the fulfillment of the prophetic words in Psalm 22. Darkness had covered the land for 3 hours, and this cry was uttered at the end of that period. We read in 1 John 1:5, "God is light." Light can have no fellowship with darkness. The cry of our Lord from the accursed tree is the expression of His response to that time of darkness. God had turned away from His beloved Son. His holy nature cannot have fellowship with evil, and Christ was "made sin for us" in that darkness. No longer could a holy God have fellowship with One who was at that very moment taking the sinner's place, becoming the sinner's substitute. The darkness therefore signified that God had turned away from His Son. Because He was the well-beloved of the Father, He could say, "My God, My God!" Yet in that awesome time while His fellowship with the Father was broken, Christ was bearing our sins in His body on the tree.

21.   What does the apostle Paul mean when he says in 2 Corinthians 5:16 "Wherefore, henceforth know we no man after the flesh; yea, though we have known Christ after the flesh, yet now henceforth know we Him no more"? (2 Corinthians 5:16).

We can be certain that when Paul said, "... though we have known Christ after the flesh yet now henceforth know we Him *no more*" he did *not* mean that he had suddenly lost his knowledge of Christ as Savior and Lord. Rather, he knew Him now in a different, spiritual way.

People had known Christ during "the days of His flesh," while He was here on earth. They had associated with Him when His designation was "Jesus of Nazareth." They had walked with Him, shared meals with Him, and wept with Him.

But mankind does not know Christ in that way any longer. He has died, has been resurrected, and has ascended. He is now the Man at God's right hand. The Father has "given all things into His hands" (John 3:35). "Wherefore, God also hath highly exalted Him, and given Him a name which is above every name" (Philippians 2:9). He is glorified at the Father's side, and we can now enjoy all that He was and did. This is because we are "in Christ," seated with Him in the heavenlies (Ephesians 2:6). How much better this is than being with Him in His earthly ministry! It's even superior to seeing His miracles, as men did while He was here on earth.

The apostle's assertion was that we no longer know Christ as a flesh-and-blood human being. The Man in the glory, having "offered one sacrifice for sins forever, sat down on the right hand of God" (Hebrews 10:12). Now we know Him in this new, spiritual relationship of faith.

This is a blessed truth for believers today. We don't only know Christ as one man knows another, but we know Him on a spiritual, heavenly plane because we are born again and the new life dwells within. We are a new creation, and therefore we see Him as our Savior and loving Lord.

22. A certain false cult uses Colossians 1:15 in an attempt to prove that God created Jesus Christ. What does the phrase "the firstborn of all creation" mean?

This simply means that God's Son has taken His place in creation. In it He holds the position of pre-eminence over every created thing—temporal, spiritual, visible, and invisible. Because the word "first" refers to station or rank, it means that Christ is the head of all creation. Most certainly, this reference does not mean that Jesus Christ is a created being.

23. Please explain 1 Peter 3:19-21.

> By whom also He went and preached unto the spirits in prison.
> Who at one time were disobedient, when once the longsuffering of God waited in the days of Noah, while the ark was preparing, in which few, that is, eight souls, were saved by water;
> The like figure unto which even baptism doth also now save us (not the putting away of the filth of the flesh, but the answer of a good conscience toward God), by the resurrection of Jesus Christ.

The term "Spirit" in verse 18, which is also the antecedent of the phrase "by whom" (or which) that begins verse 19, is the key word to the interpretation of this passage. How did Christ preach "to the spirits [now] in prison"? He did this by the Spirit. When did this preaching or proclamation occur? It was in the days of Noah, while "the ark was preparing" and while "the longsuffering of God waited." Remember the testimony of the Lord Himself at that time: "My Spirit shall not always strive with man" (Genesis 6:3). This passage therefore does not mean that Christ went into hades to offer salvation to the wicked dead, or to declare that the sacrifice had been provided. This message of warning was preached by the Spirit of Christ through Noah to the debased people of his day who are now imprisoned spirits. Those people went on in their disobedience, were swept away by the flood, and are now those "spirits in prison."

24. Did Jesus Christ really take upon Himself the guilt of our sins? If so, how could He have been a sacrifice "without spot or blemish"?

Jesus Christ was certainly a perfect sacrifice, for we are redeemed "with the precious blood of Christ, as of a lamb without blemish and without spot" (1 Peter 1:19). He was "holy, harmless, undefiled, separate from sinners" (Hebrews 7:26). But we are also told that "He [God] hath made Him [Christ], who knew no sin, to be sin for us" (2 Corinthians 5:21). The Lord Jesus not only bore our sins in His own body on the tree (1 Peter 2:24), but He took to Himself also the guilt of those sins.

You see, no man in himself can stand before God accepted and justified. Someone else must take his guilt and condemnation. Jesus Christ, Himself sinless, did exactly that for us in His substitutionary death. This is beautifully shown in Leviticus 16 by the two goats presented on the day of atonement. One was offered as a sin offering; the other was led away into the wilderness, never to be seen again. Over the scapegoat's head, Aaron was to confess "all the iniquities of the children of Israel, and all their transgressions in all their sins" (Leviticus 16:21).

25. Does Matthew 4:1 teach that the Lord Jesus was tempted by the devil? According to James 1:13,14, wouldn't it be blasphemy to say that Christ was tempted? How do you harmonize those two passages?

There is no question whatsoever that Christ was indeed tempted; first in the wilderness, then in Jerusalem, then on a high mountain. The great enemy of God met the Anointed One of God in an intense moral conflict. On that occasion, Satan's subtlety and cunning were in use as perhaps never before or since. Yet our Lord overcame him by the sword of the Spirit, the Word of God. To deny the fact of this temptation would be to reject the record of God Himself concerning His beloved Son.

Read James 1:13,14. "Let no man say when he is tempted, I am tempted of God; for God cannot be tempted with evil, neither tempteth He any man; but every man is tempted, when he is drawn away of his own lust, and enticed." This passage, as you can readily see, has nothing to do with the temptation of the Lord Jesus. Rather, it is talking about God, making the point that He is so pure that He can neither tempt nor be tempted. It was not the Father who tempted Jesus; it was Satan, the prince of this world. But he found in Christ no area of weakness; no hope of success. So he retired from the conflict in defeat.

CHRISTIAN LIFE

26. A reader of our literature wrote: "You used Psalm 37:5 as a Scripture text. It gives us the command,'Commit thy way unto the Lord.' Would you explain the mechanics of making that commitment?"

I believe that the secret of living a life of commitment to the Lord is to yield to the leading of the Holy Spirit. The key factor is in the will, at the point of choosing between the way of God and the enticements of the world, the flesh, and the devil. We know that we are committed to the way of the Lord when our decisions are for Him and against the self-life.

The principle is expressed clearly by the apostle Paul in his epistle to the Romans: "I beseech you therefore, brethren, by the mercies of God, that ye present your bodies a *living sacrifice*, holy, acceptable unto God, which is your reasonable service" (Romans 12:1). I feel that the same principle is stated in Romans 6:13, "Neither yield ye your members as instruments of unrighteousness unto sin, but *yield yourselves unto God,* as those that are alive from the dead, and *your members* as instruments of righteousness unto God."

The committed Christian surrenders himself to the Lord, relinquishing to Christ the control of his life. We do this by simply acknowledging Jesus Christ as Lord of our lives. James M. Gray is quoted as saying, "There is one thing any Christian can do. He can yield."

Surrendering to Christ profoundly affects our attitude toward the Bible. Whenever we find within its pages words of exhortation, principles to be followed, or specific commands to be obeyed, we will submit to them and *do* them. As we do, the ways of God will become an integral part of the very fabric of our lives.

Whenever, by an act of the will, we surrender the direction of our lives into the hands of Him who bought us with the shedding of His own blood, we can be confident that we are committing our "way unto the Lord."

27. **What did Jesus mean in Matthew 8:22 when He told a disciple, "Follow Me, and let the dead bury their dead"? (See also Luke 9:59,60.)**

At first it seems cruel for Christ not to let a person attend his father's funeral. After all, the death of a parent is one of life's major adversities. But in both of these passages, the question of discipleship is in view.

We must become familiar with the customs of the Middle East to understand Jesus' statement. When the potential disciple said, "Lord, permit me first to go and bury my father," he did not mean there had been a death in the family. He was saying that he would attend the obligation of custom to remain with his father until he died. But many years might pass before that happened.

Christ spoke harshly because no doubt another relative could have attended to the father until he died. The man was undoubtedly using this as an excuse to stay at home and refusing Christ the priority of life He demanded.

"Let the dead bury their dead." The issue is priorities. The spiritually dead can look after the burying of the physically dead. Christ was emphasizing that the disciple was to be first and finally committed to the orders of his Master. This must take precedence above all else. Jesus also said, "He that loveth father or mother more than Me, is not worthy of Me; and he that loveth son or daughter more than Me, is not worthy of Me" (Matthew 10:37).

28. **What did the Lord Jesus mean when He said that a man who follows Him should "take up his cross daily"? (Luke 9:23).**

First of all, let me assure you that taking up a cross is not the shouldering of some unpleasant duty or the bearing of some heavy sorrow. Any conscientious man of the world could do something like that. Taking up the cross in the biblical sense is possible only for a Christian.

In New Testament days, when a man was seen carrying a cross, people knew he was condemned and on his way to execution. The Lord Jesus therefore used this graphic figure of speech to communicate a twofold significance. First, regarding *the man himself,* he was as good as dead. It would be just a matter of time before his life ended. He had no recourse. Second, concerning *the world,* he was done with it. It was all behind him. He would be leaving it soon.

The apostle Paul was speaking of this in a spiritual sense when he wrote, "I am crucified with Christ: nevertheless I live; yet not I, but Christ liveth in me ..." (Galatians 2:20). And in Galatians 6:14, he said, "But God forbid that I should glory, except in the cross of our Lord Jesus Christ, by whom the world is crucified unto me, and I unto the world."

Now, the difficulty is having this death to self and the world become a daily, practical reality in our lives. We are to be identified with the rejection and death of the Lord Jesus. As His disciples, we are bound to the Lord in love. We are to follow Him regardless of the consequences. The apostle therefore stated, "... and the life which I now live in the flesh I live by the faith of the Son of God, who loved me and gave Himself for me" (Galatians 2:20).

29. **Please give me your interpretation of Galatians 5:19-21. I accept it literally, which means I believe that a person who professes Christ but continues drinking is not saved.**

In this passage the apostle Paul listed a number of "works of the flesh." The text reads:

Now the works of the flesh are manifest, which are these: adultery, fornication, uncleanness, lasciviousness,

Idolatry, sorcery, hatred, strife, jealousy, wrath, factions, seditions, heresies,

Envyings, murders, drunkenness, revelings, and the like; of which I tell you before, as I have also told you in time past, that they who do such things shall not inherit the kingdom of God (Galatians 5:19-21).

Among this list is drunkenness, and Paul clearly stated that "they who do such things *shall not inherit* the kingdom of God."

If I were to select the most important word in that sentence, it would be "do." It is from the Greek term *prasso*, which means, "to practice." Paul is not speaking here of the infrequent, unusual, compulsive act, but the habitual practices, the manner of life that characterizes a person.

He therefore is not saying that anyone who is guilty of drunkenness cannot be saved. Nor is he suggesting that a Christian who stumbles and commits this sin may be lost. Rather, he is making it unmistakably clear that one who makes it a *practice* of getting drunk will not inherit the kingdom of God.

Paul had just set down a catalog of sins he called "the works of the flesh." They are motivated by lust and the love of self, and are acts of disobedience to the will of God. The habitual practicing of any one of these sins, therefore, marks the person as one who will not inherit God's kingdom.

30. Please give me an explanation of the statement in 1 Corinthians 7:14 about children being holy.

The statement in question is, " . . . else were your children unclean, but *now are they holy."* The meaning begins to come clear when we consider the Old Testament background. Under the law, if an Israelite married a Gentile who practiced idolatry, the Israelite was profaned by it. He was "made unclean." The children of that union were also "unclean," and they were therefore shut out from the privileges that belonged to obedient children of Israel in their unique relationship to God.

But this is *not* the case under grace. We read in 1 Corinthians 7:14 that the unconverted husband is "sanctified" by the believing wife; conversely, a non-Christian wife is "sanctified" by her believing husband.

This means that the unsaved marriage partner, by virtue of being wed to a Christian, is brought into a sphere of influence where God's blessing abides. That one is therefore "sanctified" or "set apart," with the hope that he or she will be won to Christ.

The children of such a union are likewise not unclean but "holy." They too are "set apart" in a position where-they are in close contact with God's blessing. This is not an inward condition; it's an outward circumstance of favor.

The apostle is saying that the children of the marriage of a Christian and an unbeliever are in a place of privilege as long as either mate does not "put away" (separate from, or divorce) the other. Even if the believer should leave and have custody of the children, the possibility of winning them for Christ diminishes. If that Christian, as a follower of the Lord Jesus, is not able to sustain the marriage, then very likely the child will doubt the reality of that parent's faith. But if the children go with the unsaved mate, the believer's influence and the spiritual advantage are entirely lost.

31. Who are the people in 1 Peter 4:6 that are "judged according to men in the flesh, but live according to God in the spirit"?

The context makes it clear that Peter was *not* talking about the spirits of the dead hearing the gospel in another world. Rather, he was speaking about people who had heard the message of salvation, accepted it, and then had died—some as martyrs. The apostle was writing to believers who were currently being persecuted, and was encouraging them by referring to men and women who had already gone to Glory. He declared that the gospel was preached to those saints who are now dead for a twofold purpose: (1) "that they might be judged according to men in the flesh," and (2) that they might "live according to God in the spirit."

The first phrase, "that they might be judged according to men in the flesh," means that one of the reasons they received the good news of salvation was so that they might glorify God by bearing reproach while they were yet alive. Wicked men who pursued a life of sensuality, lust, drunkenness, and abominable idolatries (v. 3) condemned these believers and were able to bring about the death of some of them. But God knew this would happen when they were saved, and He planned that they should exalt Christ through steadfastness in the midst of persecution.

The second phrase, "but live according to God in the spirit," is an assertion that these believers are now in Heaven, enjoying a life related to God in the spirit—ever-lasting and indestructible. The teaching is this: when people are saved, they may experience bitter persecution here, but they will inherit eternal glory over there.

32. In Psalm 51, David confessed his sin to the Lord and prayed, "Restore unto me the joy of Thy salvation" (v. 12). Was he asking God to save him again? If so, is a believer lost whenever there is unrepented sin in his life?

The answer to both of these questions is a resounding NO! David was *not* asking for a return of his salvation, but the restoration of its joy. In great distress of soul because of his sin, he was seeking the delight of fellowship with God once again.

Think about it a minute. If unconfessed sin caused believers to be lost, no Christian could ever be sure of Heaven. The least transgression in thought, word, or deed would change our standing before God. We could be saved and lost a hundred times a day.

The apostle John wrote, "My little children, these things write I unto you, that ye sin not. And if any man sin, we have an advocate with the Father, Jesus Christ the righteous; and He is the propitiation for our sins..." (1 John 2:1,2). Christ's sacrifice for our sins satisfied God's wrath. It remains in effect continuously for believers. That satisfaction is the basis of our standing with the Lord, and it cannot be altered by an individual sin. Therefore, our transgressions are not charged as guilt against us.

When believers do sin, however, Christ is our lawyer and advocate. He "goes to bat for us" so that our fellowship with the Father can be restored. The child of God also needs the application of the "water of the Word" to bring him cleansing, self-judgment, and confession.

The propitiation of Christ is sufficient and efficacious for every believer. We read of the Lord Jesus that "by one offering He hath perfected forever them that are sanctified" (Hebrews 10:14). Though the joy of fellowship with God may be lost because of unconfessed sin, the believer's standing before God is not changed. He is still saved. On the basis of his union with Christ, he is still God's child.

CIRCUMCISION

33.   Did Paul have a double standard in the practice of circumcision? A comparison of Acts 15:23-25 and 6:1-3 seems to indicate this.

No, a double standard is not involved here. Paul did not believe that circumcision was necessary for a believer's salvation nor for his obedience. The question that arose in Acts 15 originated with the members of a sect called the Pharisees. They said that "it was needful to circumcise them Gentile believers, and to command them to keep the law of Moses" (Acts 15:5). Paul's practice regarding circumcision is stated clearly in 1 Corinthians 9:20,22, which says in part, "And unto the Jews I became as a Jew, that I might gain the Jews; to them that are under the law, as under the law . . . that I might gain them that are under the law. . . . I am made all things to all men, that I might by all means save some." Paul had Timothy submit to this rite for the purpose of reaching the Jews, as is stated in a phrase of Acts 16:3, ". . . because of the Jews."

The apostle was consistent with his own philosophy of evangelism.

CLOTHING

34. **Leviticus 19:19 says, "Neither shall a garment mixed of linen and woolen come upon thee." Does this mean we are not to wear garments of mingled fibers?**

Remember, these regulations were given by the Lord to His covenant children, the Jews. They were primarily established so that Israel would be a distinct and separate people. Surrounded as they were by heathen nations, they were to be "unmixed" in heart and practice. They were taught this by precept and commandment in every area of life.

These regulations came to an end when the law was fulfilled in Christ. The New Testament contains no regulations for Christians about the mixing of fabrics in their clothing.

35. **Would you please explain how Christians should view the Old Testament law in Deuteronomy 22:5? How does this relate to women wearing men's clothing today?**

The woman shall not wear that which pertaineth unto a man, neither shall a man put on a woman's garment; for all that do so are abomination unto the Lord thy God (Deuteronomy 22:5).

If Deuteronomy 22:5 is a regulation for Christian women in this dispensation, the church age, then the other requirements found in this same chapter must also be observed. For instance, verse 10 says, "Thou shalt not plow with an ox and an ass together." Additional instructions on clothing are found in verse 11, "Thou shalt not wear a garment of different sorts, as of woolen and linen together." We encounter some strange difficulties when we take what was given by God to the nation of Israel and try to make it apply to New Testament believers. (Please read the next paragraph!)

Several passages in the New Testament do give instructions for Christian women relating to dress. First Timothy 2:9 exhorts women to "adorn themselves in modest apparel, with godly fear and sobriety." And the apostle Peter said a number of things about feminine apparel (see 1 Peter 3:1-3).

Godly women will dress to please God and to show that they are willing to obey Him. Any mode of dress that destroys the sweet, God-given quality of femininity, or that breaks down the God-ordained characteristics of the sexes, should cause a Christian lady to evaluate carefully her apparel.

COMMANDMENT

36. **In Romans 7 the apostle Paul used the term "the commandment" six times. The word "commandment" is in the singular. Is there a special commandment to which this has reference?**

No. Paul did use the commandment "Thou shalt not covet," but only as an example of what he was teaching. He was speaking of the law, showing that it is the "commandment," the law, which reveals the exceedingly sinful character of sin (Romans 7:13).

CONTENDING FOR THE FAITH

37. **When Jude wrote in his epistle about "contending for the faith" (v. 3) to what faith was he referring?**

Jude was speaking of the whole body of revealed truth contained in the writings of the Holy Scriptures. He was not referring to personal faith, therefore, but rather to the entire revelation from God in His Word. Luke 18:8 also speaks of the "faith," as do Romans 1:5; 2 Corinthians 13:5; and other passages. "The faith" is the total scope of Christian doctrine, without deletion or addition, as infallibly given in the inspired words of the biblical authors. This revelation through the Holy Spirit includes all the vital doctrines of Christianity. In fact, the main tenets of "the faith" are found right in the book of Jude. I therefore suggest you read the entire epistle.

CORNELIUS

38. Was Cornelius a Christian before Peter came to tell him about salvation?

The story is recorded in Acts 10. Though Cornelius was said to be a "devout" man, this simply means that he had a pious attitude toward God. He was so religious that he even prayed to the God of Israel. He also "gave much alms to the people," an act of charity that was probably directed to the people of Israel. No doubt he had been attracted by the simple monotheism of Jewish worship. But none of this indicates that he had been saved by grace. The clinching statement is found in Peter's recounting his experience. Cornelius told him that an angel had commanded him to send for Peter, "Who shall tell thee words, by which thou and all thy house shall be saved" (Acts 11:14). Cornelius' salvation came through hearing and believing the Word as brought by Peter. Until that time he was not a Christian.

CREMATION

39. What should be the attitude of the Christian toward cremation? Do the Scriptures give the believer permission to use this method for the disposition of the body?

As far as I know, cremation is not suggested anywhere in the Scriptures. The general impression we receive from the Bible, however, is that burial is the proper way for the dead body to be disposed of.

Some have thought that Leviticus 20:14 and 21:9 give justification for the act of cremation. But an examination of these passages indicates that both of these were

God-ordained judgments for those who had willfully disobeyed God's laws under the levitical system.

But one might say, "What about King Saul? Weren't the bodies of him and his sons burned after they were killed in battle?" Yes, they were. But this does not indicate Divine approval. The inhabitants of Jabesh-gilead may have been strongly influenced by pagan traditions. In no way could their custom be counted as an example for believers.

Moreover, the language of 1 Corinthians 15 suggests that a body goes into a tomb, whether it be a plot in the earth or a grave in the sea. "It is *sown* a natural body" (1 Corinthians 15:44).

Whenever the disposition of a body is mentioned in the Bible, burial is the mode. God said to Adam, ". . . for dust thou art, and unto dust shalt thou return" (Genesis 3:19). No reference is ever made to "ashes."

DEATH AND HELL

40. Does Ephesians 4:9 teach that Christ descended into Hell?

No, it does not. The verse reads, ". . . He also descended first into the lower parts of the earth." Bible students are not agreed as to the meaning of these words, but none of them teach that they speak of an actual descent into Hell. Some believe that this refers to the time between our Lord's death and resurrection in fulfillment of the messianic prophecy of Psalm 16:10. *The King James Version* rendering "Thou wilt not leave my soul in hell" is wrong. The editors of the *New Scofield Reference Bible* were right in changing the word from "hell" to "sheol." The Greek equivalent is "hades"—"the place of the dead." Prior to the resurrection of Jesus Christ, this abode of the departed spirits was divided into two sections—a place of torment, and Abraham's bosom (Luke 16). I believe that when the Lord Jesus arose, He led all of the redeemed souls out of that portion of hades and into Heaven. The lost are still in the place of torment. Revelation 20 tells us that "death and hades are cast into the lake of fire. This is the second death." The Bible does not say that the Lord Jesus "descended into hell," but rather "into hades."

41. Please explain why some translations use the word "hades" in place of "hell" as the King James Version renders it.

The reason for this change, as it appears in the *New Scofield Reference Bible* and other versions, is that the King James translators did not reflect the difference in the meaning of the words *hades* and *gehenna* in the Greek.

The term *hades,* strictly speaking, does not refer to the final state or place of the unsaved, but has to do with the condition of the wicked after death while awaiting resurrection for judgment. The only possible exception is Matthew 16:18, where Jesus said that the "gates of hades" would never overcome His church. Some take this particular phrase to be a reference to hades as the headquarters of satanic opposition to the church. Others see it as a simple declaration that death will not finally overcome believers, for all who have trusted Christ will receive everlasting life and be resurrected.

The word *gehenna,* however, never speaks of death itself, nor does it depict man's state between death and resurrection. It appears only 12 times and is always properly rendered "hell." The lost who have died are now in *hades* awaiting resurrection and judgment, after which they will be cast into *gehenna,* the final abode of the unbelieving dead. To show this distinction, most versions have gone to the transliteration of the word *hades* whenever it occurs in the Greek New Testament.

DEMON POSSESSION

42. Please clarify Acts 16:16,17. How could the young woman speak the truth if she was demon-possessed?

And it came to pass, as we went to prayer, a certain maid possessed with a spirit of divination met us,

who brought her masters much gain by soothsaying.
The same followed Paul and us, and cried, saying,
These men are the servants of the Most High God,
who show unto us the way of salvation.

Satan sometimes seeks to align himself (in the eyes of
people) with the work of God. To do this, he transforms
himself "into an angel of light" (2 Corinthians 11:14).
Certainly it was strange that this demon-possessed maid
should speak truthfully about Paul's witness. It was an act
of deception, however, to draw the multitudes to her
prophesying. You will remember the time when demons
even witnessed to the fact that our Lord was the Holy One
of God though men were scoffing at the truth. Like his
Lord, the apostle Paul refused to ally himself with Satan,
and he commanded the demon to come out of the girl.

EGYPT

43. **Ezekiel 29:12-16 speaks of the desolation of
    Egypt for 40 years and the return of the
    Egyptians afterward. Has this prophecy been
    fulfilled or is it still future?**

This prophecy has been fulfilled. The pharaoh mentioned
in this passage was probably Pharaoh Hophra, who cap-
tured Gaza (Jeremiah 47:1). He was overthrown by
Nebuchadnezzar, as the Bible records in Jeremiah 43:10-
12; 44:30. This pharaoh boasted that not even a god
could defeat him. The extent of his conceit is framed in
verse 3 of Ezekiel 29.

When he was conquered by Nebuchadnezzar, Hophra
was strangled by his own soldiers. Then, after 40 years of
desolation and dispersion, the Egyptians were restored to
their land, but they never again became a dominant
nation. The prophecy of Ezekiel 29:14 has been true,
"they shall be there a base [or subordinate] kingdom." The
40 years of Egypt's desolation ended when the Babylonian Empire was destroyed by the Persians. In Isaiah 19
we read of a future restoration of Egypt, but even then she
will be subject to Israel.

ELIJAH

44. Will you please explain Malachi 4:5,6? Is this prophecy yet to come, or has it been fulfilled?

Behold, I will send you Elijah, the prophet, before the coming of the great and terrible day of the Lord;
And he shall turn the heart of the fathers to the children, and the heart of the children to their fathers, lest I come and smite the earth with a curse (Malachi 4:5,6).

The event described here is still future. I personally believe that the prophet Elijah will return to this earth to prepare the way for the Messiah. He may be one of the two witnesses mentioned in Revelation 11.

Just as John the Baptist came "in the spirit and power of Elijah" (Luke 1:17) to "prepare the way of the Lord" (Luke 3:4) at His first coming, so Elijah the prophet will appear on earth prior to the glorious return of the Lord Jesus. His assigned task will be to prepare a remnant in Israel for the Messiah's coming.

45. Malachi 4:5 predicts the coming of Elijah the prophet before "the great and terrible day of the Lord." Matthew 17:10-13 seems to indicate that Elijah has already come in the person of John the Baptist. Please explain.

And His disciples asked Him, saying, Why then say the scribes that Elijah must first come?
And Jesus answered and said unto them, Elijah truly shall first come, and restore all things.
But I say unto you, That Elijah is come already, and they knew him not, but have done unto him whatsoever they desired. Likewise shall also the Son of man suffer of them.
Then the disciples understood that He spoke unto them of John the Baptist (Matthew 17:10-13).

You will find in Matthew 17:11,12 a definite and distinct reference to both the appearance of John the Baptist in the fulfillment of the prophecy of Malachi 3:1 and a future appearance of Elijah in the fulfillment of Malachi 4:5,6. Neither is excluded by our Lord's words. Quite often in the writings of the Old Testament prophets, both the first and second advents of Christ are predicted within the same paragraph. These men saw two mountain peaks of prophecy on the same horizon, and yet they did not see that there was a valley or space of time between them. In Malachi 3:1, therefore, the coming of "My messenger" is foretold. This was the ministry of John the Baptist at Christ's first advent. But a "messenger of the covenant" was also predicted. This is the Lord Jesus coming "suddenly to His temple." Verses 2 through 5 indicate His second advent and the accompanying judgment.

Luke 1:17 states that John the Baptist ministered *in the spirit and power* of Elijah. Jesus said, "Elijah is come already, and they knew him not" (Matthew 17:12). He was speaking of John the Baptist. But He also said, "Elijah truly shall first come" (Matthew 17:11). This statement refers to a time yet future.

ETERNITY

46. What is the meaning of Matthew 24:35, which says, "Heaven and earth shall pass away, but My words shall not pass away"?

The first part of Christ's statement refers to the fact that when time ends and eternity begins, the earth and its planetary system will be completely renovated by fire. In Peter's second epistle we read that the atmospheric heavens "shall pass away" and the earth "shall be burned up" (2 Peter 3:10). This does *not* mean that the earth will pass out of existence, as some mistakenly affirm on the basis of certain Scriptures which say it will "perish." Remember, the word "perish" is often used in a context where it does not mean annihiliation. When Peter spoke of the flood of Noah's day, for example, he said that the world "perished." But it did not go out of existence. He went on to say that the next time the earth is purged, it will be by fire. The elements will be dissolved, but we have the promise that the new heaven and earth will emerge out of the roaring furnace of flame. John described this spectacular scene: "And I saw a great white throne, and Him that sat on it, from whose face the earth and the heaven fled away, and there was found no place for them" (Revelation 20:11). Later he added, "And I saw a new heaven and a new earth; for the first heaven and the first earth were passed away, and there was no more sea" (Revelation 21:1).

Yes, this material world in which we live will undergo a radical transformation, but through it all God's Word will abide unaltered. His character cannot change; neither can His Word. This is what Jesus meant by the statement recorded in Matthew 24:35.

EVANGELISM

47. Matthew 24:14 is often quoted as the incentive for hurrying to finish the task of world evangelism. Is it true that the Lord Jesus will come just as soon as the gospel is preached to all nations?

> And this gospel of the kingdom shall be preached in all the world for a witness unto all nations; and then shall the end come   (Matthew 24:14).

Our Lord's coming for His church, even as His return to establish His kingdom, will be at the "appointed time." He appeared "in the fullness of time" in the first advent; the same will be true of His second coming. No work of man can hasten His return.

As with all Scriptures, these words of Matthew 24:14 must be interpreted in the light of their context. The major portion of Matthew 24 and 25 is descriptive of the tribulation period, particularly the final 3 and 1/2 years. The "gospel of the kingdom" is the proclamation that the King, Jesus Christ, is returning to defeat Antichrist and establish His millennial reign. It will be heralded by the preachers of the kingdom, the 144,000 sealed ones of

Israel. Their ministry will occur *after* the church has been taken to Heaven in the rapture. God will ordain this company of evangelists from restored Israel with the task of giving the kingdom testimony to all nations.

When the work of proclaiming this gospel of the kingdom has been accomplished, the tribulation will end, Antichrist will be defeated at Armageddon, Satan will be chained for 1,000 years, and the Lord Jesus Christ will set up His promised reign of peace and righteousness over all the earth.

EXTINCTION OF THE HUMAN RACE

48. With all the talk about overpopulation and pollution, I wonder if the human race will ever die out. What about nuclear war? Do you think man could destroy himself by bombing or by radioactive fallout?

The answer is NO! Ever since the dawning of the nuclear age, we've heard predictions that a total holocaust could consume the race and wipe out all civilization. In this decade some pessimistic environmentalists have pointed out that the earth's capabilities to support life are limited and will someday run out. Others are fearful that the pollution of the atmosphere or oceans might reach a saturation point, and that all living creatures including man would perish.

But we who follow the Scriptures can be certain that there will be no extinction of the human race! The Lord Jesus did speak of a future time of great tribulation, the likes of which this world has never seen. Terrible judgments will fall upon the earth in a fearful outpouring of God's wrath upon the unrepentant nations. It will result in the death of one-third of the world's population (Revelation 9:18). But the race will not be totally destroyed. In fact, Christ said that those days will be shortened so that people can be spared (see Matthew 24:22).

Some of the judgments of the endtime could possibly include the unleashing of nuclear weapons. Peter indicated that this could be the case when he wrote that "the day of the Lord will come as a thief in the night, in which the heavens shall pass away with a great noise, and *the elements shall melt with fervent heat;* the earth also, and the works that are in it, *shall be burned up"* (2 Peter 3:10).

Christians need not fear those dreaded days, for before these judgments break loose, the church will be caught up to meet Christ in the air. We'll be raptured! Ours is the joyful expectation of seeing the Lord and being forever with Him; not the excruciating end of the human race.

FALLING FROM GRACE

49.   You say that a genuine believer cannot fall out of favor with God and lose his salvation. Then how do you explain Galatians 5:4, "... ye are fallen from grace"?

You have not quoted all of the verse. In entirety it says, "Christ is become of no effect unto you, whosoever of you are justified by the law; ye are fallen from grace" (Galatians 5:4). After looking carefully, I'm sure you'll conclude that this text does not mean what many are reading into it—that a Christian can disqualify himself from the grace by which he was saved, and ultimately be lost again.

You must remember the situation confronting the Christians in Galatia when Paul wrote this letter. They were being troubled by Judaizing teachers, legalists who were telling them that in order to have salvation they must be circumcised, keep the law of Moses, strictly observe the Sabbath, and comply with a host of other ordinances.

Is that how a sinner is saved? Absolutely not! The apostle has already said in this letter, "But that *no man is justified* by the law in the sight of God, it is evident; for, The just shall live by faith" (Galatians 3:11). Never, NEVER can a person stand before God justified by the deeds of the law! No ritual, no ceremony can save. Paul wrote, "For by grace are ye saved through faith; and that not of yourselves, it is the gift of God—not of works, lest any man should boast" (Ephesians 2:8,9).

Now read the text again. "Christ is become of no effect unto you, *whosoever of you are justified by the law;* ye are fallen from grace." This verse simply means that a person who tries to keep the law to satisfy the demands of God's holiness, and thereby earn salvation, in actuality has turned away from trusting in God's grace. He has turned his back on the Lord's abundant and free provision in Christ and has gone back under the law. In this sense, therefore, he has "fallen from grace," but he has not become unsaved. Rather, he never was saved. When confronted with the teaching of God's grace, he fell back into the natural man's idea that salvation is earned by works.

50.   Please interpret Hebrews 6:4-6. Does this passage teach that a person who has been saved can "fall away" and lose his salvation?

Let me answer your second question first. No, these verses do *not* teach that a truly saved person can become lost again. I suggest you read this entire passage carefully (Hebrews 6:1-12). The word "therefore" in verse 1 points back to chapter 5, verses 12 through 14, the section which I believe gives the key to this passage.

> For when for the time ye ought to be teachers, ye have need that one teach you again the first principles of the oracles of God, and are become such as have need of milk, and not of solid food.
> For everyone that useth milk is unskillful in the word of righteousness; for he is a babe.
> But solid food belongeth to them that are of full age, even those who by reason of use have their senses exercised to discern both good and evil (Hebrews 5:12-14).

The writer clearly is speaking of true believers, and he is *not* talking about losing their salvation. The subject of verses 4 through 6 of chapter 6 is *repentance,* not salvation. He did not say, "It is impossible . . . to renew them again unto *salvation";* but rather, "unto repentance."

As I see it, the author of Hebrews was talking about people who had been saved for quite some time and had made progress in their Christian growth. But they had grown cold spiritually; they had "lost their first love." Instead of becoming mature (the word "perfection" in verse 1 means "to bring to maturity"), they had lapsed into spiritual infancy. The apostle Paul gave a similar warning to Corinthian believers who were not growing.

> If any man's work shall be burned, he shall suffer loss; but he himself shall be saved, yet as by fire (1 Corinthians 3:15).

Hebrews 6:4-6 is therefore not a warning about the danger of losing salvation, but of chastening. Believers in Christ can fall short of God's purpose. They may even continue on in disobedience until His chastening hand falls upon them, perhaps even to the extreme of physical death. John supported this when he said,

> If any man see his brother sin a sin which is not unto death, he shall ask, and he shall give him life for them that sin not unto death. There is a sin unto death; I do not say that he shall pray for it.
> All unrighteousness is sin, and there is a sin not unto death (1 John 5:16,17).

This is not a matter to be taken lightly. I urge you to take careful heed to the conclusion of the admonition, "That ye be not slothful, but followers of them who through faith and patience inherit the promises" (Hebrews 6:12).

Every Christian ought to feed upon the Word, to grow in grace, and to go on to maturity. Every unconfessed sin should be openly dealt with and put away, lest the discipline of God come. Compare 1 Corinthians 9:24-27, where again the subject is not salvation but service, and the loss is not of redemption but reward.

GOD

51. I never doubt any part of the Bible, but sometime I can't figure out what it means.

Here is an example: "And the Lord repented
that He had made Saul king over Israel"
(1 Samuel 15:35). What does the Bible
means when it says that God repented?

This is a good question. The same expression appears in Genesis 6:6, "And it repented the Lord that He had made man on the earth." Does this mean that God had made a mistake? Or that He had committed some sin He needed to repent for? Of course not! God does not commit errors, nor does He ever need to correct some faulty action He has taken.

When the word "repent" appears in the Bible, it means "a change of mind." When it applies to God, it is being used as a figure of speech. He is presented in terms that apply to man so that we can understand what is meant. Language has been formed for human use. God's being and actions are beyond our full comprehension; therefore, they must be expressed in man's terminology.

How else could the author of 1 Samuel, or Moses in the Pentateuch, have expressed the idea? It's the only way we can comprehend the meaning. The term "God repented" is not used to indicate that some personal sin needed confessing; nor does it imply a serious error in action or judgment that required correction. Rather, it may be defined as the "aroused emotions of God which prompt Him to a different course in dealing with people."

Phrases like this can be confusing, especially to the beginning Bible student. But if you will do a little research or ask someone more experienced to help you, you will find that the Scriptures are not contradictory. There is a good reason for expressions like this.

52. First John 4:12 and John 1:18 both say, "No man hath seen God at any time." However, in reading Exodus 24:10,11, I found the phrase, "they saw the God of Israel." Please explain.

We know, of course, that there are no contradictions in the Word of God, the Bible. This is, as you have stated correctly, a "seeming" one. It is true that no man hath seen God; that is, in His very essence, His spiritual being. However, John went on to say in John 1:18, "... the only begotten Son, who is in the bosom of the Father, He hath declared Him."

We must conclude, then, that the occasions when God was "seen" in the Old Testament were pre-incarnate appearances of the Lord Jesus Christ. Remember, Isaiah said that he "saw also the Lord" (Isaiah 6:1). But, we learn from John 12:37-41 that the One whom Isaiah beheld was Christ, the second person of the trinity. I therefore believe that Moses, Isaiah, and the children of Israel saw a pre-incarnate manifestation of the eternal Son, not the very essence of God the Father.

53. Will we see God the Father and the Holy Spirit in Heaven, or only the Lord Jesus?

Scripture has not given us a definite answer to this question. Some references indicate that both Father and Son will be seen. Daniel 7:13,14 speaks of both the "Son of man" and the "Ancient of days," referring, I believe, to the Father and Son. Revelation 5 depicts a scene in Heaven where both appear: the Father is sitting upon a throne holding a scroll, and the Lamb (the Lord Jesus) takes the scroll out of His right hand. Some Bible scholars believe that we will see only the Son, in whom "dwelleth all the fullness of the Godhead bodily" (Colossians 2:9). Let us await that time, fully expectant that our entire beings will be totally satisfied with what we see.

54. Please discuss Genesis 6:1-6. Who were the "sons of God" referred to in this passage?

Some Bible scholars believe that the "sons of God" in Genesis 6 were descendants of the godly line of Seth who had disobeyed the Lord by intermarrying with the wicked line of Cain. Personally, however, I take the expression to mean "angels."

Only by a divine act of creation can any being be called a "son of God." Adam is called a "son of God" in Luke 3:38, for he was created by God. Christians are "sons of

God" because they have the new nature by a creative act of God (2 Corinthians 5:17; Ephesians 2:10; John 1:13).

Angels are called "sons of God" in the Old Testament; in fact, wherever the phrase is used, it refers exclusively to angels (Job 1:6; 2:1; 38:7; Psalm 29:l; 89:6). There is no reason to make the expression mean anything different in Genesis 6. Therefore, these are angels who fell from their first estate. Their sin was, as Jude 6 and 7 states it, "in like manner" as the sins of Sodom and Gomorrah. These fallen ones cohabited with the "daughters of men," and from that wicked union came an offspring of giants. These *nephilim* were evil men of great stature and terrible wickedness. The flood was sent as judgment to destroy them.

This sentence from the note in the *New Scofield Reference Bible* may be helpful: "Whichever view is held, it is obvious that Satan attempted so to corrupt the race that the Messiah could not come to redeem man." God preserved Noah and his family, and thereby kept a line through which the Lord Jesus would come. Genesis 6:9 indicates that Noah and his family were the only ones who escaped the corruption that brought the judgment of the flood upon the race.

55. Why did God give the order in 1 Samuel 15:3 that Saul should "utterly destroy all that they have, and spare them not; but slay both man and woman, infant and suckling, ox and sheep"?

This command was issued because of Amalek's opposition to the Israelites when they entered the promised land.

On various occasions God used His people Israel to punish the nations round about them. His command to "go and smite Amalek, and utterly destroy" was judgment upon a wicked king and his subjects. They had refused to repent of the sin of hindering the people of Jehovah. The Amalekites were still the adversaries of God, and the order for their destruction was an object lesson of the Lord's wrath upon sin.

HANDS

56. **Do we have scriptural authority today for the "laying on of hands" that was practiced in apostolic times?**

It appears from the New Testament record that "laying on of hands" had three usages:

1. *Christian Fellowship* (Acts 6:1-7). The apostles "laid hands" on the seven men chosen by the church to care for earthly affairs. In like manner, the elders of the church at Antioch "laid hands" on Paul and Barnabas as they were "sent forth by the Holy Spirit" (Acts 13:1-4). It appears to me that fellowship is suggested by this act in both cases. The apostles expressed their fellowship with the church in Jerusalem in choosing deacons. The elders in the church at Antioch showed the fellowship of the church with Paul and Barnabas as they embarked upon their missionary journeys.

2. *The bestowal of the gift of the Holy Spirit*. This no doubt was done to show the authority of the disciples at the time the Samaritans received the gift of the Holy Spirit through the laying on of hands by Peter and John (Acts 8:17). It could be that this was used to avoid any contention in the future about which was the original church (consider what our Lord said in John 4:20).

Another instance is recorded in Acts 19:6 when the disciples of John acknowledged the authority of the apostle Paul.

3. *The receiving of the gift of God* (2 Timothy 1:6). The presbytery or elderhood joined Paul when he performed this act (1 Timothy 4:14). Apparently the laying on of hands was practiced only by the apostles, for we have no record in the New Testament of their passing on to others the authority to do this.

Every believer receives the Holy Spirit simultaneously with conversion. The Spirit today gives gifts, "dividing to every man severally as He will" (1 Corinthians 12:11). The Bible does not teach apostolic succession, nor has the laying on of hands continued from the apostolic age.

57. **I have been seeing more and more Christians raise their hands to God as part of their worship. Is this practice scriptural? If not, how do you explain 1 Timothy 2:8?**

I will, therefore, that men pray everywhere, lifting up holy hands, without wrath and doubting.

The New Testament mentions "lifting up hands" in only two locations, and in both instances it is done during prayer. The first occurs in Luke's account of the ascension. We are told that the Lord Jesus "... led them out as far as to Bethany; and He lifted up His hands, and blessed them" (Luke 24:50).

The second reference is 1 Timothy 2:8, the passage in question. Paul wrote, "I will, therefore, that men pray everywhere, lifting up holy hands, without wrath and doubting." In this chapter Paul was telling men and women how to act properly in the public assembly of believers. In verse 9, however, he was speaking of the women. Audible prayer is designated in verse 8 as the responsibility of men. The text reads literally, "I will, therefore, that *the* men pray ...." *Note the definite article,* which indicates that he was speaking of the male members of the congregation. He would turn his attention to the women's behavior in church in the next verse.

The emphasis of Paul's exhortation about prayer is not upon the physical act of the raising of hands but upon the condition of the heart. The hands to be lifted in prayer must be "holy hands." If a man is going to lead the congregation before the throne of grace in a public service of the church, his heart must be right before God. His life is to be marked by true piety, or he is to refrain from praying before the assembly.

I do not find anywhere in New Testament teaching to the church either a command for the raising of hands in public worship or a prohibition of this practice. Paul's admonition to Timothy contains neither; rather, it expresses God's requirement that the men who lead in public prayers before the congregation are to be faithful men whose lives are marked by piety and obedience.

HEAVEN

58. How can we be perfectly happy in Heaven if we know that some of our loved ones are not there?

We often forget that relationships will be entirely different in Heaven. One of the greatest joys on earth is a wholesome, loving family. But we reason in terms of the finite, and pleasure is often based upon the response of the senses. In Heaven, however, we will be delivered from all the limitations of the flesh (1 Corinthians 13:12). The family circle will not be reestablished. Oh, certainly we will have reason to remember and rejoice in the blessings of God's love to us while on earth; surely we will know one another in Glory. The source of our joy, however, will be the person and presence of our blessed Lord. Luke 20:35,36 teaches that the marriage relationship will not be resumed in Heaven. Even our bodies will be different, as 1 Corinthians 15:44 makes clear. Therefore, be careful not to think of the causes for earthly happiness as the same for heavenly joy. We will have an enlarged perspective, for we will view everything in the light of eternity.

59. Please discuss the meaning of Revelation 22:14.

A literal translation of this verse is, "Blessed are they that wash their robes...." This states the great qualification for entrance into the eternal city. Men do not go in by works but by cleansing. You see, God demands absolute holiness of all who enter Heaven.

But how is a man made fit for the presence of the Almighty? All men need a twofold washing. In Revelation 7:14, John spoke of those who "have washed their robes...." He used the aorist tense, which speaks of once-for-all action. This occurs when we place our trust in Christ and God declares us forgiven and righteous in Him.

The second washing is a daily cleansing through confession of sin, in accordance with 1 John 1:9. The apostle has reference to this "washing" in Revelation 22:14, for he uses the present durative which means, "Blessed are they that *keep on washing* their robes." Even if the rendering, "that do His commandments," is held to be the correct translation of the verse, the requirement for entering Heaven is still not changed. Only those who "have been washed in the blood of the Lamb" will be allowed to enter the City. They are the ones who "keep and do His commandments," and who walk daily in obedience and confession of sin.

HOLY SPIRIT

60. In 2 Thessalonians 2:7 the Bible speaks of the Holy Spirit being "taken out of the way." Does this mean that He will be taken completely out of the world?

For the mystery of iniquity doth already work;
only He who now hindereth will continue to hinder
until He be taken out of the way (2 Thessalonians
2:7).

I believe that the person designated by the pronoun "He" in this verse is the Holy Spirit, although the Scripture quoted does not explicitly state this. The personal pronoun is used in reference to the Divine Being numerous times in the Bible (see Philippians 1:6; Hebrews 10:37). Certainly the Holy Spirit, resident in the church of the Lord Jesus Christ, has been restraining iniquity down through the centuries. We are not to conclude, however, that the Holy Spirit will be taken out of the world, or, as the verse says, "out of the way." God the Spirit is omnipresent, so He will still be here. But He will not be operating in the same way He indwells the church during this age. The words "until He be taken out of the way" may be translated literally, "until out of the midst He be." This means that He will no longer be active as the one who restrains the outworking of lawlessness. This "departure" will occur at the rapture of the church.

61. Please explain God's taking His Holy Spirit from King Saul. Does "once in grace, always in grace" apply to every dispensation?

During the present age, when the Holy Spirit is resident in every believer, He is here to "abide with you forever" (John 14:16). He does not depart, though at times He is "grieved" (Ephesians 4:30). In the Old Testament, however, His activity was quite different. The Spirit would come upon men for special service. In 1 Samuel 11:6, we read that "the Spirit of God came upon Saul." He would also depart from men; and in the case of Saul, both in 1 Samuel 18 when he was angry at David and in chapter 28 when he consulted the witch of Endor, the Spirit of God left him.

62. What did the Old Testament saints know about the work of the Holy Spirit?

In reading the words of John 7:39, ". . . the Holy Spirit was not yet given," some have thought that the Holy Spirit did not come into the world until Pentecost. They therefore suppose that the children of God in Old Testament times knew nothing about the work of the Spirit. But this conclusion overlooks such key passages as Job 32:8; Psalm 139:7; Isaiah 11:2. Old Testament saints knew:

1. That He was the author of life. Elihu said, "The Spirit of God hath made me, and the breath of the Almighty hath given me life" (Job 33:4). Moses recorded in Genesis 1:2, "The Spirit of God moved upon the face of the waters." Speaking of animals, the psalmist declared, "Thou sendeth forth Thy Spirit, they are created" (Psalm 104:30).

2. That He revealed God's will through His servants in the Old Testament. Numbers 27:18 records, "and the Lord said unto Moses, Take thee Joshua, the son of Nun, a man in whom is the Spirit." David realized this when he cried, ". . . take not Thy holy Spirit from me" (Psalm 51:11). The prophet Ezekiel testified, "Then the Spirit entered into me, and set me upon my feet, and spoke with me" (Ezekiel 3:24).

3. That He was the teacher of God's people in the Old Testament. Nehemiah 9:20 records, "Thou gavest also Thy good Spirit to instruct them." (See also Proverbs 1:23.)

4. That the Holy Spirit endued man with power for service. Micah 3:8 gives this witness, "But truly I am full of power by the Spirit of the Lord." The word of the Lord to Zerubbabel was, "Not by might, nor by power, but by My Spirit, saith the Lord of hosts" (Zechariah 4:6).

5. That He gave them joy and peace (read Psalm 51:11,12).

6. That the Spirit could transport the children of God from earth to Heaven (1 Kings 18:12).

The Holy Spirit was very active among men in Old Testament days, and men and women were aware of His power and influence.

IDLE WORDS

63. Just what are the "idle words" our Lord spoke of in Matthew 12:36?

> But I say unto you that every idle word that men shall speak, they shall give account of it in the day of judgment (Matthew 12:36).

As with all other Scripture, these words must be considered in context. The Pharisees had accused Christ of doing His mighty works in the power of Beelzebub, or Satan. This was blasphemy, and it demonstrated their totally depraved condition. The Lord Jesus scathingly rebuked them, saying, "For out of the abundance of the heart the mouth speaketh" (v. 34). Their words had revealed the evil, unregenerated state of their hearts.

Judgment awaits all who display their rebellion and wickedness by their words. What a man says even in idle, unthinking moments is therefore important. Teenagers and young people must be especially careful how they speak of God or Christ. A reverence, a holiness must attend their speech. Consider Romans 10:9,10, "That if thou shalt confess *with thy mouth*...," and "... with *the mouth* confession is made unto salvation."

ISRAEL

64. Revelation 1:7 says, " . . . every eye shall see
Him, and they also who pierced Him . . . ."
How is it possible for those who crucified
Christ to be present when He returns?

This seeming impossibility is explained by Zechariah, "I
will pour upon the house of David, and upon the inhabitants of Jerusalem, the Spirit of grace and of supplica-
tions; and they shall look upon Me whom they have
pierced . . ." (Zechariah 12:10). The prediction of Revelation 1:7 does not refer specifically to the men of Christ's
day who crucified Him, but to the nation of Israel. The
word "they" refers to the nation, not the actual partici-
pants in the execution of Christ.

65. Will Israel live in the promised land during
eternity? Where will she be after the
millennium?

We do know that Israel will possess the promised land and
live in it during the 1000-year earthly reign of Jesus
Christ. And most Bible scholars feel that in eternity she
will dwell in the New Jerusalem, pointing to Revelation
21:12 as evidence. Some, however, maintain that Revelation 21 describes the heavenly city of the millennial age,
and not the New Jerusalem during the eternal state. But it
really makes little difference, for whoever inhabits that
city for the 1,000 years will abide there for eternity. Some
evidence for this viewpoint is found in the experience of
Abraham. Dwelling in the New Jerusalem is very likely
the realization of his hope, as recorded by the author of
Hebrews. "For he looked for a city which hath founda-
tions, whose builder and maker is God" (Hebrews 11:10).
We may conclude, therefore, that Israel will dwell in the
New Jerusalem in eternity.

66. Matthew 8:12 is hard for me to understand.
Please explain the meaning of the phrase

". . . the sons of the kingdom shall be cast out into outer darkness . . . ."

The book of Matthew is primarily the gospel that presents Christ as King. The key is found in the first verse, "The book of the genealogy of Jesus Christ, *the son of David, the son of Abraham*" (Matthew 1:1). Remembering this along with the setting of the words in Matthew 8 will help us interpret correctly what our Lord said.

A centurion, a Roman captain, asked Jesus to "speak the word only, and my servant shall be healed." Though this man was a Gentile, he was doubtless a believer in the Lord Jesus Christ. Christ had been presenting Himself to Israel as their King. Two chapters later, He instructed His disciples, "Go not into the way of the Gentiles, . . . but go, rather, to the lost sheep of the house of Israel" (Matthew 10:5,6). It was therefore unusual for a Gentile to come to Him and with so much trust that Christ said, "I have not found so great faith, no, not in Israel" (v. 10).

From this demonstration of faith the Lord Jesus projected His thoughts to a time and dispensation about to dawn, the church age. He spoke of that time when God would "visit the nations, to take out of them a people for His name" (Acts 15:14). He described an era when many would enter the kingdom from the east and the west to fellowship with Abraham, Isaac, and Jacob.

Now, who were the *natural* children of the "kingdom"? The people of Israel who rejected Christ. These natural children, the "sons of the kingdom," would be cast out for their refusal to acknowledge Christ as King.

This is exactly what has happened and will happen. In unbelief, Israel rejected the King and crucified Him. The pronouncement of the judgment to come upon them is found in Matthew 23:38, "Behold, your house is left unto you desolate."

The same truth is presented in Romans 9 through 11 by the apostle Paul. Quoting Isaiah, he wrote, "I was found by them that sought Me not; I was made manifest unto them that asked not after Me. But to Israel He saith, All day long I have stretched forth My hands unto a disobedient and contrary people" (Romans 10:20,21). Gentiles have turned to God in faith and received the grace, while Israel has refused to believe and experienced judgment. "Because of unbelief they [the Jews] were broken off, and thou standest by faith" (Romans 11:20).

The "sons of the kingdom" of Matthew 8:12 are therefore those Jewish individuals who rejected the Lord Jesus when He came to earth. He presented Himself to them, the people of God with the kingdom promises, as their true Messiah. He confirmed His claim with countless miracles. But they would not have Him. This persistent unbelief led to their individual rejection, and God set aside the nation of Israel during the church age.

67. Please explain John 12:40. Why would God purposely harden the hearts of the Israelites so they could not understand?

He hath blinded their eyes, and hardened their heart;
that they should not see with their eyes, nor
understand with their heart, and be converted, and I
should heal them (John 12:40).

Christ is here quoting the prophecies found in Isaiah 6:9,10 and 53:1. The prophet saw the unbelief of the nation of Israel which would culminate in the rejection of their Messiah. Though they had been the recipients of His miracles and had heard His words of warning, they continued in their refusal to obey His word. God therefore sent judicial blindness to Israel, a hardening to their hearts. This is God's prerogative. Because He is sovereign, He is perfectly just in punishing the ungodly. So we read in Romans 11:25 "That blindness in part is happened to Israel, until the fullness of the Gentiles be come in."

Having resisted God's warnings, denied Christ's miracles, and finally rejected their Messiah, Israel was punished with a judicial blindness. Jehovah had pleaded with Israel, "For I have no pleasure in the death of him that dieth...;wherefore, turn yourselves, and live" (Ezekiel 18:32). But Israel would not turn, so God judged the nation by blinding their eyes and hardening their hearts. They had reached the place where "they could not believe" (John 12:39).

68. Was it God's will for His chosen people to resort to war to accomplish His plan for them? In other words, did God sanction war?

The words of the Lord through Moses to Israel were these: "And thou shalt do that which is right and good in the sight of the Lord, that it may be well with thee, and that thou mayest go in and possess the good land which the Lord swore to give unto thy fathers, to cast out all thine enemies from before thee, as the Lord hath spoken" (Deuteronomy 6:18,19). Deuteronomy 7 follows with the command that Israel should smite these seven nations of Canaan and "utterly destroy them; thou shalt make no covenant with them, nor show mercy unto them" (Deuteronomy 7:2). This makes it quite clear that God intended for His chosen people to fight against these nations to carry out His plan. God's design included Israel's possession of the land He had given her—a land inhabited by these pagan nations.

Israel was to be a separate people. The Canaanites were degraded; their iniquity was full (Genesis 15:16). So a holy God ordered the complete extermination of the idolatrous nations in Canaan, that Israel might remain a separate people. Through Abraham and his descendants the one true God was to be manifested to the world. Israel, therefore, was not to be polluted and ruined by the licentiousness of the heathen nations.

> But thus shall ye deal with them: ye shall destroy their altars, and break down their images, and cut down their idols, and burn their carved images with fire.
>
> For thou art an holy people unto the Lord thy God; the Lord thy God hath chosen thee to be a special people unto Himself, above all people who are upon the face of the earth (Deuteronomy 7:5,6).

JERUSALEM

69. Would you explain Luke 23:31, "For if they

> do these things in a green tree, what shall be
> done in the dry?" (Luke 23:31).

Jesus was on His way to Calvary when He spoke these words to a group of women who were following Him, weeping out of pity. Moved by their tears, but knowing their grief was superficial, He tenderly warned them about the coming destruction of Jerusalem and the terrible suffering that awaited the Jewish people. The sentence "For if they do this in a green tree, what shall be done in the dry?" is a proverb that was popular at the time. He meant, "If the Romans will sentence an innocent man to crucifixion when God has not yet set aside His chosen nation and it is living in passive submission to the empire, what will they do when God abandons Israel and the Roman government declares the people guilty of rebellion?" The Lord's dire prediction of terrible oppression for the Jews was partially fulfilled in A.D. 70 and 135, and it will be fully realized during the great tribulation. But thank God, through this future adversity Israel will repent, and the "dry" tree shall once again become "green."

70. Who are the nations and kings of the earth in Revelation 21:24?

John was describing the eternal home of the redeemed. He presented the universal aspect of the New Jerusalem by saying that Gentiles will be among its citizens. The Greek word *ethne,* rendered "nations," should be translated "Gentiles." The apostle John mentioned the "kings of the earth" to depict the preeminence of this heavenly city. These men, who held important positions upon earth will bring the glory and honor of these offices into their new home. This passage therefore speaks of saved individuals in the eternal state.

71. Is the New Jerusalem going to be shaped like a pyramid, or will it be like a cube?

Revelation 21:15-17 gives us the dimensions of the city. The length and breadth of the New Jerusalem are equal, which makes it square in shape. However, we are also told that the height is the same, and that each of the three dimensions is 12,000 furlongs. A furlong is equal to 660 feet, so the measurement for each dimension is more than 1500 miles. Some do think the city will be a cube, while others believe it will be a pyramid with sloping sides and the peak being set at the height given. Of one thing we are sure: the "glory of God" will light it, and the Lamb will be the "lamp of it" (Revelation 21:23).

JEWS AND SAMARITANS

72. Why were the Jews and Samaritans enemies?

When the kingdom of Israel was taken captive by the king of Assyria, the cities of Samaria were populated by a number of heathen people who were brought in to help colonize the land. Some Israelites, however, remained. Therefore, as time went on, the Samaritans became a mixed people (see 2 Kings 17:24-33). The animosity between the Jews and Samaritans probably resulted from the fact that Samaria and Jerusalem became rival capitals. In addition, because the temple was in Jerusalem, a rivalry of religion also developed (John 4:20). After the Jews returned from exile and rebuilt their temple in Jerusalem, the Samaritans constructed their own place of worship on Mount Gerizim. The resulting hatred continued for centuries, and was still strong during the time of our Lord's earthly ministry.

JONAH

73. Would you please express an opinion on the authenticity of the story of Jonah?

Read carefully these words of the Lord Jesus Christ: "For as Jonah was three days and three nights in the belly of the great fish, so shall the Son of man be three days and three nights in the heart of the earth" (Matthew 12:40). Now read Luke 11:29-32. To question the authenticity and historicity of the account of Jonah is to question the truthfulness of Jesus Christ, and thus cast doubt upon His omniscience as God the Son.

JUDAS

74. Was Judas buried in the potter's field? Can this plot of ground be identified today?

The Bible does not specifically tell us that Judas was buried in the potter's field. In Matthew 27:3-10 we read the story of the remorseful Judas throwing the 30 pieces of silver on the floor of the temple. The record states that the priests used the money to buy a potter's field, a place to bury aliens and paupers. Matthew also declared that Judas went out and hanged himself. We are quite certain he did this before the priests purchased the field.

Acts 1:18,19 is an explanatory parenthesis which Luke inserted in his account of Peter's message to help his readers understand the background of the apostle's statements. Luke said that Judas had purchased a field with his ill-gotten gain. We may conclude that he meant the chief priests used the money the traitor had returned to buy the field in his name.

Was Judas buried in the potter's field? We don't know. It could be that the priests purchased the very spot where Judas had committed suicide to make it a burial place for paupers, and that this is where the corpse of the traitor was interred. Luke doesn't say this, however, but simply declares that the field purchased with the 30 pieces of silver became known as *Akeldama,* which means "the field of blood." Two reasons may account for this name: (1) it was purchased with the blood money received for the betrayal of Jesus Christ, and (2) it was connected with the tragic death of Judas, either indirectly through its purchase with the tainted money, or because Judas died there.

75. Do you think Judas could have changed his mind and not have betrayed the Son of God? If he

had, would not that have made the Bible untrue regarding Judas?

Judas was a free moral agent, and he chose to reject the Son of God. Two lines of truth are involved, as stated in the book of Acts, "Him, being delivered by the determinate counsel and foreknowledge of God, ye have taken, and by wicked hands have crucified and slain" (Acts 2:23). God delivered Him up; but man betrayed and crucified Him. Could Judas have changed his mind? A good question; but remember, he did not. God in His foreknowledge knew exactly what he would do. Judas was called "the son of perdition" (John 17:12).

It is only theoretical to ask, "IF he had...." Questions like this could be repeated many times over in relation to accounts in the Bible, but to no avail. We do have the record, and "the witness of God is greater" (Psalm 19:9). His Word is as His judgments, "true and righteous altogether." "Forever, O Lord, Thy word is settled in heaven" (Psalm 119:89).

Judas betrayed "innocent blood." The Bible records that choice and act accurately and factually. He was never a saved man, but instead was called "a devil" by our Lord Himself (John 6:70,71).

JUDGMENT

76. Where and when will the judgment seat of Christ take place? Will this judgment include all believers?

Let's take the questions one by one so that we can make our answers as clear as possible. Where? When? Who?

First, the judgment seat of Christ is located in Heaven, and we will meet the Lord there for judgment. Believers who have died—who have left their bodies to go and be "with Christ"—are described in 2 Corinthians 5:1-10. In 1 Thessalonians 4:17, we are told that all living believers will be "caught up...in the clouds, to meet the Lord in the air."

Our conviction that the judgment seat of Christ will take place in Heaven is corroborated by Revelation 19:7-9. John's vision of the "marriage supper of the Lamb" described the "wife" of the Lamb as having "made herself ready." That this preparation will take place at the judgment seat of Christ is clear from verse 8, "And to her [the church] was granted that she should be arrayed in fine linen, clean and white; for the fine linen is the righteousnesses of saints." These "righteousnesses" are the deeds of believers that have gone through the examination of the judgment and have been approved. The judgment seat of Christ, before which all Christians will appear, is therefore in Heaven.

Second, this event will occur between the rapture (1 Thessalonians 4:13-18) and the glorious appearing of Christ as Lord of lords and King of kings (Revelation 19:11-16). The great tribulation, detailed in Revelation 6 through 18, will take place on earth while the church saints are standing before the Lord Jesus to have their works tested.

Third, who will be judged here? All believers from Calvary until the rapture will appear before Christ. The people who are converted during the tribulation, of course, will not be rewarded at this time, for they will still be alive upon earth. True, many will die, but others will still survive and enter the millennial age. Those who are martyred will not be resurrected until Christ's glorious return. Daniel 12:1-3 indicates that the Old Testament saints will also be resurrected at this time.

Since "we must all appear" to give account for the "deeds done in the body," let us make certain that the motives for our actions are right. If they are, in that day when we are "made manifest," our works will remain. Not done in the strength of the flesh but in the power of the Spirit, they will stand the test of Christ's scrutiny.

77. Since the judgment seat of Christ follows the rapture of the church, won't the joy of our heavenly bliss be interrupted because we'll have to face our sins? Will it bring us shame and sorrow?

In the first question of this section, we considered the where, when, and who of this topic. This question has to do with the *what* of the judgment seat of Christ.

First, that judgment will not be a judgment for *sin.* All punishment for sin was laid upon Christ when He took our place at Calvary. Hebrews 9:26 says, "But now *once,* in the end of the ages, hath He appeared to put away sin by the sacrifice of Himself." The sin question has been settled forever! The believer can say with assurance, "There is, therefore, now no condemnation [judgment] to them who are in Christ Jesus" (Romans 8:1).

Second, that judgment will not be a judgment for *sins.* The One who was "made sin for us" also "bore our sins in His own body on the tree" (1 Peter 2:24). He "put away" *sin;* He made atonement for our *sins.* We are therefore given the positive word of Ephesians 1:7, "In whom we have redemption through His blood, the forgiveness of sins, according to the riches of His grace." The judgment of the believer's sins is past. The child of God will never be punished for them! Christ has already paid the full price.

Third, that judgment will be a manifestation of the believer's *works.* We shall not stand before our Lord as sinners, but as saints. Each believer must appear at this judgment seat, "that everyone may receive the things done in his body, according to that he hath done, whether it be good or bad" (2 Corinthians 5:10).

The body of the believer belongs to the Lord. The "temple of the Holy Spirit," it should be used in His service and for His glory (1 Corinthians 6:15-19; 2 Corinthians 4:10). We are responsible for the deeds done in the body. Our thoughts, acts, words, and service will be known, tested, and judged before Christ. "The fire shall test every man's work of what sort it is." The deeds meeting His favor, then worked in the Spirit of His glory, shall remain as gold, silver, and precious stones. Those works failing to gain His approval will go up in smoke like wood, hay, and stubble. Now read carefully Revelation 19:6-8. Is it possible that these "righteousnesses of saints" (not justifying righteousness, which is a gift) are the deeds which receive the approval of our Lord?

Having considered *what* the judgment seat will involve, we can have the assurance that we will never be faced with the sins already covered by the blood of Christ. When we stand there, it will be in our redeemed, resurrection bodies. Our understanding will be so enlightened that we shall be ready to say "Amen" to whatever takes place. A saint of another generation has said, "He will show us where and how we failed, but instead of this making us afraid of Him, it will only deepen in our souls the sense of His unchanging grace and love, that He should so long have borne with such failing, erring creatures."

78. It bothers me when people, ministers in particular, speak negatively about others in the ministry, calling attention to what they think to be their failings. Just how far should one go in judging another Christian worker? Does Mark 9:38-41 apply in this case?

Mark 9:38-41 is the record of our Lord's rebuke of sectarianism, and does apply to the question. But its primary interpretation is about the problem of the disciples' narrow view of their own little group as the "in" people.

The Bible pointedly tells us that we have the responsibility to withdraw from "every brother that walketh disorderly" (2 Thessalonians 3:6). The apostle Paul further stated, "And if any man obey not our word by this epistle, note that man, and have no company with him, that he may be ashamed" (v. 14). This passage makes it evident that Christians do have the obligation to pass judgment on the life and teachings of others.

However, I think I sense a deeper aspect of the reader's question. Believers, especially pastors, must avoid the indiscriminate criticism and harsh judgment of other Christian leaders. We would do well to heed carefully Paul's exhortation in Romans 14:4, 10-12. The solemn fact that "every one of us shall give account of *himself* to

God" (v. 12) should cause us all to be careful in judging our brothers.

The apostle Paul gave us the example of what we should do when a brother is wrong in practice or doctrine in his epistle to the Galatians. The problem was Peter's error about Christian liberty. He had slipped back into some legalistic practices. But Paul did not engage in fleshly "sniping." Rather, he withstood Peter "to the face, because he was to be blamed" (Galatians 2:11).

79. Please explain the meaning of Matthew 7:6.

> Give not that which is holy unto the dogs, neither cast your pearls before swine, lest they trample them under their feet, and turn again and lacerate you (Matthew 7:6).

Though this command of the Lord Jesus seems to stand by itself, it follows logically His warning against having a critical spirit and judging our fellowmen adversely. The obligation to avoid unfair condemnations, however, does not free us from the responsibility of being discreet in presenting the spiritual truths of God. Some people, like certain of the religious leaders of Christ's day, are antagonistic to the gospel. They may appear to be interested and ask us questions about our faith, but they are only after ammunition to use against us. We must recognize such men and refuse to enter into dialog with them.

Jesus called these people "dogs" and "swine." The apostle Peter, referring to unregenerate men trying to infiltrate the churches, told us why they deserve terrible names like these: "But it is happened unto them according to the true proverb, The dog is turned to his own vomit again; and the sow that was washed, to her wallowing in the mire" (2 Peter 2:22). Religious teachers who continue to reject Christ still love the way of sin, and they will eventually return to it. Furthermore, Jesus said they will attack the very ones who are trying to teach them the truths of God.

The words of this verse must therefore be considered in the context of the entire chapter. Christ had warned against judging others in a harsh, condemning manner. But there is another side of the coin. He also instructed us not to be taken in by those who are against Christ. "Dogs" and "swine" were considered unclean under the levitical law. Peter used these very words to describe those who have disdain and disrespect for the Word of God (2 Peter 2:22). Remember, the Lord Jesus was speaking the words recorded in Matthew 7:6 within earshot of many unbelieving Pharisees who had spurned the gospel.

The same attitude toward the enemies of God is found in Acts 13:46, where Paul and Barnabas said to some who spoke against the truth: "It was necessary that the Word of God should first have been spoken to you; but seeing ye put it from you, . . . lo, we turn to the Gentiles." No longer would the apostles "give that which is holy" unto these religious leaders, only to have them trample it under their feet.

80. Please explain John 12:47. "And if any man hear My words, and believe not, I judge him not; for I came, not to judge the world but to save the world."

Our Lord's first coming was not for the purpose of judging, but for bringing salvation. When He returns to this earth the second time, however, He will come in judgment. The rejection of His message during the 3 years of His earthly ministry did not result in His immediate action as Judge. However, Jesus plainly said in John 12:48, ". . .the word that I have spoken, the same shall judge him in the last day." The basis of the judgment to come upon those who reject the Savior, especially those who did so at the time of His first coming, will be the message He proclaimed. This is why our Lord said, "He that heareth My word, and believeth on Him that sent Me, hath everlasting life, and shall not come into judgment, but is passed from death unto life" (John 5:24).

KINGDOM

81. **If Jesus is going to establish an earthly kingdom, why did He say before Pilate, "My kingdom is not of this world; if My kingdom were of this world, then would My servants fight"? (John 18:36).**

The verse itself gives the answer. When the Lord Jesus said, "My kingdom is not of this world," He used the Greek preposition *ek,* which means "out from" and indicates origin or source. His kingdom, unlike those that are established by force or human persuasion, will come from Heaven by the power of God. Christ was in no way declaring that He would not set up an earthly reign. He was making a contrast. The kingdoms of this world come into being, rise to power, and are brought to an end by human energy and force. The words "then would My servants fight" show what His kingdom would be like if it were established by men. Christ's kingdom will come when He returns personally to usher it in. And when that occurs, it will not happen through the physical force of finite man but by His own omnipotent power.

82. **Please explain Matthew 24:40. Does it refer to the rapture?**

Then shall two be in the field; the one shall be taken, and the other left (Matthew 24:40).

In my opinion, this verse does not refer to the rapture of believers. The preceding paragraph of Matthew 24, verses 29 through 35, foretells the return of Christ with "power and great glory." Therefore, when we read in verse 36, "But of that day and hour knoweth no man," the reference is to the revelation of Jesus Christ at His second advent— not to the rapture. Verse 40 is speaking of those who are "taken" in judgment. You will observe that the Holy Spirit used the flood as an illustration (vv. 37-39). The wicked of his day "knew not until the flood came, and took them all away." Those "taken away" in the flood were experiencing the judgment of God. Noah and his family, however, were "left"—kept safe in the ark. Likewise, at the return of Christ those who will be "taken" are being removed in judgment. And those "left" are the righteous who will enter the millennial kingdom.

83. Does Matthew 22:11 refer to our entrance into Heaven? Is the wedding garment representative of salvation?

Matthew 22 actually presents two closely related parables. The first (vv. 1-10) tells of a king who prepared a great wedding feast for his son. The invited guests all refused to come, however, and murdered the servants who brought the invitation.

The second parable (vv. 11-14) is about the wedding garment.

> And when the king came in to see the guests, he saw there a man who had not on a wedding garment.
> And he saith unto him, Friend, how camest thou in here not having a wedding garment? And he was speechless.
> Then said the king to the servants, Bind him hand and foot, and take him away, and cast him into outer darkness; there shall be weeping and gnashing of teeth.
> For many are called, but few are chosen (Matthew 22:11-14).

These two parables are not about Heaven, but about the millennial kingdom the Lord Jesus will establish here on earth when He returns at the close of this present age.

The words, "Friend, how camest thou in here not having a wedding garment? ...Bind him hand and foot, and take him away, and cast him into outer darkness..." (vv. 12,13) could *never* be said to a sinner saved by grace and already in Heaven. A person must be clothed with Christ's righteousness before he can enter Glory.

Philippians 3:9 says that righteousness "is of God by faith." We receive it at the moment of salvation, and it can never be taken away.

Of the *earthly* kingdom, however, we are told that the angels "shall gather out of His kingdom all things that offend, and them who do iniquity" (Matthew 13:41). A number of passages in the gospel of Matthew tell us who will be excluded from the kingdom:

Matthew 22:11—the mere professor, the one who says he is a Christian but who has never trusted Christ.

Matthew 24:48—the evil servant.

Matthew 25:8-12—the unwatchful professor.

Matthew 25:30—the unprofitable servant.

The parable of the missing wedding garment therefore refers to people of the millennial kingdom. It does not speak of believers who have entered Heaven.

LAST DAYS

84. Do the terms "last day" and "last days," used repeatedly in the Bible, mean the same thing?

The meaning can be determined only by treating each occurrence individually. The "last days" foretold of Israel in Isaiah 2:1-5 are the days of restoration, blessing, and exaltation of God's chosen nation. They pertain specifically to the millennium, the final phase of Israel's history. Similar passages that deal with Israel's "last days" are Jeremiah 30:18-24; Daniel 10:14; Micah 4:1-8.

The Bible also contains predictions of the "last days" of the church. In particular, Hebrews 1:2 indicates that the "last days" began with the first advent of Christ. Within this present age, and especially near its close, is another period called the "last days" or "last times" that is marked by apostasy (see also 1 Timothy 4:1-3; 2 Timothy 3:1-8; 2 Peter 3:1-9; Jude 17-19).

I believe the "last days" for Israel will include the "time of Jacob's trouble," culminating in the restoration of the Jews at the end of the tribulation and the beginning of the 1000-year reign of the Lord Jesus. The "last days" for the church will conclude with the rapture of the saints, when our Lord comes "in the air." The "last day" (singular) refers to the time of resurrection, especially of believers (John 6:39,44,54).

MARY

85. According to Luke 1:5, Elisabeth was a Levite. Since she was a cousin of Mary, does this make Mary a Levite? I was of the opinion that Mary was a descendant of David, and was of the tribe of Judah.

Mary was indeed a descendant of David and of the tribe of Judah. The genealogy given in Luke is probably Mary's lineage, and traces our Lord's ancestry from David through Nathan. On her father's side, Elisabeth was "of the daughters of Aaron." It is possible, however, that on her mother's side she was of the house of David. History shows that those two families often intermarried.

MILLENNIUM

86. Do Ezekiel 43, 45, and 46 teach that blood sacrifices will be resumed during the millennium? How does this harmonize with Hebrews 10:6 and 8?

These chapters in Ezekiel do clearly state that the sacrifices and offerings will be reinstituted during the millennium. There will be an important difference, however. They will no longer be *shadows* of the great sacrifice of Christ, but *memorials*. The resumed temple worship with the sacrifices will commemorate Christ's offering, just as the Lord's supper is a memorial for us now.

The relationship of Israel to God in the millennium will be quite different from that of believers today. However, the *basis* of Israel's relationship will be the same as ours. In all dispensations, the atoning death of Christ is the only means of attaining peace with God.

In the kingdom, Israel will not be in the body of Christ as members of the church are now. They will be an earthly people of flesh and blood, enjoying abundant earthly blessings and prosperity. Theirs will be an earthly order of worship, and the sacrifices will be part of this order.

In reference to the Hebrews passage, God certainly did not "have pleasure" in the burnt offerings themselves as a means of approaching Himself. His pleasure is in the Son of His love, and in the sweet-smelling savor of His acceptable sacrifice.

87. During Christ's future 1000-year reign, will anyone die as a result of judgment?

Yes, they will. Isaiah 11:4 states, "...He shall smite the earth with the rod of His mouth, and with the breath of His lips shall He slay the wicked." This means that any act of rebellion against Christ the King during the millennium will result in immediate physical death. Note also Isaiah 65:20, "...but the sinner, being an hundred years old, shall be accursed." (See also Isaiah 66:24; Jeremiah 31:29,30; Zechariah 14:16-21.)

MONEY

88. What are the scriptural methods of raising money for the Lord's work?

The scriptural means of supporting the work of the gospel is by the freewill offerings of the Lord's people (read 1 Corinthians 9; 16:1,2; 2 Corinthians 9:9; Galatians 6:6; Philippians 4:15-19). All other ways are unscriptural and often become carnal.

89. In Luke 16:1-13, did the unjust steward expect the debtors to pay the other half of their debt at another time? If not, how could the master commend him?

We must keep in mind the fact that the Lord Jesus often gave parables to emphasize only one point. In this instance, He was discussing the proper use of money in its relationship to the future. The unjust steward, a son of this age, acted shrewdly. Therefore, he received the commendation of his master, even though his employer had suffered financial loss. But notice: the master did not approve his *act.* Rather, he only commended *him,* and this was probably for his cleverness in providing for the future.

Our Lord gave this parable to teach that it is important for His followers to apply their material wealth to eternal investments that will result in the salvation of souls. This is the way "to lay up treasure in Heaven." If we do, then when we reach Glory, many will be there to welcome us as we enter the "everlasting habitations." The unjust steward resourcefully prepared for his own future. The Lord Jesus exhorted believers to use their earthly property to make eternal friends.

90. Please explain Deuteronomy 14:26. I read this verse recently and do not understand it.

> And thou shalt bestow that money for whatever thy soul desireth: for oxen, or for sheep, or for wine, or for strong drink, or for whatsoever thy soul desireth; and thou shalt eat there before the Lord thy God, and thou shalt rejoice, thou, and thine household (Deuteronomy 14:26).

When you study the context, you note that this occurs in the section instructing about the tithe the Israelite was to bring to the place "which the Lord thy God shall chose to set His name." That place, of course, was the tabernacle.

If the worshiper was unable to carry the tenth of the fruit of his field and flock to the tabernacle because of the distance, he was required to sell it and take the money to the prescribed place of worship. There he could purchase with the money the things mentioned in the verse, and use them to celebrate before the Lord.

I do not know why God permitted the purchase of wine and strong drink for the celebrating. Be sure of this, however, the Word of God is unmistakably clear in forbidding the abuse of wine.

This secondary offering was consumed at the sanctuary with joy and praise to God by the person whose land or flock was tithed. I do not presume that this verse condones the use of liquor. Some things in God's dealings with His people Israel must remain unexplained until that day in His presence when we shall fully understand.

NEW NAME

91. In Revelation 2:17 and 3:12 a "new name" is mentioned. Can you explain this to me?

He that hath an ear, let him hear what the Spirit saith unto the churches: To him that overcometh will I give to eat of the hidden manna, and will give him a white stone, and in the stone a new name written, which no man knoweth except he that receiveth it (Revelation 2:17).

Him that overcometh will I make a pillar in the temple of My God, and he shall go no more out; and I will write upon him the name of My God, and the name of the city of My God, the new Jerusalem, which cometh down out of heaven from My God; and I will write upon him My new name (Revelation 3:12).

The first reference is of a "new name written, which no man knoweth except he that receiveth it." Then, in Revelation 3:12, the Lord Jesus said, "I will write upon him the name of My God and,...My new name." The name engraved on a white stone (2:17) suggests something indelible, permanent—something of glory and brilliance. Of course, a *name* always represents the character, the nature of the person whose name is used. The second reference indicates that the Lord's own name is placed upon the bearer. The one who bears that name will have an intimate knowledge of it. Whose name could bring more honor, reward, distinction to the child of God than the name of the Lord? These words of Christ may tie in with this: "I have declared unto them Thy name, and will declare it" (John 17:26). Only in eternity will we have the full knowledge of His name.

ORDINANCES

92. Are the ordinances of baptism and the Lord's supper to be continued during the entire church age?

Some believers say that these ordinances were of a temporary character, to be practiced only until the church was established. The witness of church history, however, is that the ordinances were practiced continuously. More important, Paul, "the apostle to the Gentiles," taught a group of men in the Gentile city of Ephesus and baptized them when they believed (Acts 19:1-7). Then too, when Cornelius the Roman and his household believed, Peter "commanded them to be baptized in the name of the Lord" (Acts 10:48). Neither of these were on "Jewish ground."

The command for keeping the Lord's supper is given with the words "till He come" (1 Corinthians 11:25). We are to remember His death until we see Him face to face.

93. Do the bread and wine in the Lord's supper really become the body and blood of Christ, or are they merely emblems? Explain the statements in John 6:53-58.

I do not believe the Scriptures teach that the bread and wine of the communion service become the actual body and blood of Christ. Nothing magical occurs when we partake. The elements are only symbols.

If you read all of John 6 carefully, you will see that the Lord Jesus was not speaking literally about eating His flesh and drinking His blood. Nor was He talking about the Lord's supper. The subject of His discourse was life. The key to the passage is verse 63, "It is the spirit that giveth life; the flesh profiteth nothing. The *words* that I speak unto you, they are spirit, and they are life."

We "feed" upon the living Christ by receiving and believing His Word. We appropriate Him by faith through the Bible.

To believe that the bread and wine actually become our Lord's body and blood is to place the participant in a position of "cannibalism," and I am sure Christ did not teach that. Those who hold this doctrine, called "transubstantiation," believe that when the priest blesses the wafer and the cup, they actually become the body and blood of Christ. If one interprets Matthew 26:26-29 in this way, he must conclude that at the last supper with His disciples, Jesus somehow broke His own body in His hands. That's ludicrous! The bread and the wine are therefore figurative. They represent His broken body and shed blood.

Our Lord said in Luke 22:19, "This do...." For what purpose? "...in remembrance of Me," or "for calling Me to mind." The reason for the use of the bread and wine is clearly stated here. It is a "remembrance," a commemoration of Him who is not present. That the elements cannot actually be His flesh and blood is also taught in I Corinthians 11:26. Read this verse several times. We *remember* His death, we *memorialize* it. But we worship and serve a risen, living Lord.

94. Please explain 1 Corinthians 11:27-29.

The believer who participates in the Lord's supper unworthily is one who has failed to acknowledge that the bread is a symbol of the body of the Lord Jesus, which was broken at Calvary in death for us, and that the cup represents His blood, shed for our sins. If a Christian does not understand and respect this when partaking of the Lord's supper, he has participated unworthily. He has not practiced self-judgment, and dishonor has been done to the body and blood of the Lord. Furthermore, if we eat and drink without self-judgment, the Lord will judge or chastise us. This is what was happening in Corinth, and the result was sickness and even death for many believers.

95. Is the Lord's supper for us today? Or did it belong to the Jews only and not to the Gentiles, as some have claimed?

Our Lord instituted this memorial feast for all who are members of His body called the church. The apostle Paul was given a special revelation of "the mystery" not made known in former ages; that is, the church. In

1 Corinthians 11:23-26, he repeated the words of our Lord, "This do in remembrance of Me." He was writing to the Corinthian assembly, composed of Jews and Gentiles who were saved by grace. The words "till He come" are conclusive proof that the Lord's supper is to be celebrated during this present age by all who believe in Christ.

PARABLES

96. Who are represented by the five foolish virgins in the parable of Matthew 25:1-13? Did they once have oil that gave light?

Chapter and verse divisions sometimes confuse rather than clarify the interpretation of a passage. Keep in mind that chapter 24 gives detailed teaching about the tribulation and the glorious second advent of the Lord Jesus. Chapter 25 continues that theme. Nothing in either portion refers to the rapture, the "catching away" of the church. Though much of the teaching of this Scripture passage may be applied today in establishing spiritual principles, the strict interpretation limits the latter portion of chapter 24 to Christ's return to the earth.

The parable of the virgins (25:1-13) continues to discuss events related to Christ's visible return. The topic is the coming of the Bridegroom *with* His bride at the close of the tribulation ((24:29,30). If you have a Bible with marginal renderings, you will note that Matthew 25:1 reads, " . . .who took their lamps, and went forth to meet the bridegroom *and the bride*." Further, in verse 10 you read, "They that were ready went in with Him *to the marriage feast*." The "*marriage feast*" follows the "marriage," which already will have taken place in Heaven.

Who then are the virgins? Certainly not the church: for the church (the bride) will be returning with the Lord Jesus. Rather, they are Jewish disciples who have professed to believe on Christ. All of them go forth to meet the Bridegroom. Those without oil, though professing their interest in the coming Bridegroom, will be shut out of the marriage feast. Throughout the Word of God, oil is symbolic of the Holy Spirit. I repeat, this passage has to do with Jews at the end of the tribulation who profess to be disciples, and who are awaiting the return of the Lord Jesus Christ.

97. Please explain Mark 4:25. Does this sound fair to you?

For he that hath, to him shall be given, and he that hath not, from him shall be taken even that which he hath (Mark 4:25).

This verse is illustrated by the parable of the pounds (Luke 19:11-26). The principle involved is that of rewards. The one who is unfaithful to the Lord will not only be denied recompense, but he will also forfeit what he already has. On the other hand, faithfulness will produce rich benefit and will put a believer in the position to receive additional commendation from the Lord.

PAUL

98. Recently in our city a Bible teacher asserted that the apostle Paul was not married. What does the Bible say about this?

The Bible does not say, and we therefore do not know. Luke indicated in Acts 26:10 that prior to Paul's conversion he was possibly a member of the Sanhedrin. The word "voice" in the *King James Version* should be translated "vote." If Saul of Tarsus was a voting member of that body, he no doubt was married and had children, because this was one of the qualifications for membership in the Sanhedrin. If Paul was married, his wife was not living when he wrote his first letter to Corinth. The possibility that Paul was a widower may be indicated in 1 Corinthians 7:8.

PERISH

99. Does the word "perish" in John 3:16 have the same meaning as our English word today "to become extinct" or "become destroyed"? How do you harmonize this with the unrighteous being assigned to "everlasting punishment"? (Matthew 25:46).

These two expressions are not in conflict. Actually, the word "perish," as used in John 3:15,16 means "to lose utterly." The idea is not "extinction" but "ruin or loss, not of being, but of well-being" (W. E. Vine). If you trace the use of this word in the New Testament, the meaning becomes clear. In Luke 5:37 the word is used in speaking of the destruction of wineskins. In Luke 15:4,6 it describes lost sheep; that is, they are lost to the shepherd. The apostle John records that Jesus used it to denote the spoiling of food (John 6:27).

The Bible does not teach annihilation. After the body dies, the soul lives on. For both believer and unbeliever, it is eternal. I presume the questioner has this in mind. Numerous passages in the Bible speak of "torment," "punishment," and similar ideas of conscious suffering for the unrighteous. Revelation 20:10 speaks of the "lake of fire," the final abode of the unregenerate. The devil and the beast and the false prophet will be cast into it, and they "shall be tormented day and night forever and ever."

A notable example of life after death for the unbeliever is our Lord's account of the rich man in Luke 16. Possessed of his faculties, including speech, hearing, seeing, feeling, this wealthy person said, "I am tormented in this flame" (Luke 16:24). This was no extinction, no annihilation. But it was suffering, torment, and conscious agony.

PHYSICAL APPETITES

100. Please explain the phrase in 1 Corinthians 6:13, " . . . and the Lord for

the body." Does this refer to physical healing?

Foods for the body, and the body for foods; but God shall destroy both it and them. Now the body is not for fornication, but for the Lord; and the Lord is for the body (1 Corinthians 6:13).

This verse has nothing to do with bodily healing as some Bible students suppose. It can be understood only when we recognize that Paul was using two simple illustrations to teach that Christian liberty is applied differently to the human appetite for food than for sexual desire.

Eating is a function necessary for the maintenance of life. The stomach and food were made for one another. But, Paul said, all physical functions cease at death—both the stomach and food are no longer needed. Therefore, eating is not a moral issue in itself. It acquires spiritual significance only when abused through gluttony or connected with heathen ceremonies.

The body, however, is not destined to destruction, but to transformation and glorification (Philippians 3:21). The body therefore has special significance to the Lord. God did not design the body for fornication as He did the stomach for food. Not sexual indulgence, but fellowship with the Lord is essential for the perfect functioning of the body.

The body, then, is to be the vehicle through which we serve the Lord ("but for the Lord"). It can fulfill this purpose only through His enablement ("the Lord for the body").

In summary, this verse disproves the claims of some that the appetites for food and sex are on the same level.

POLYGAMY

101. Why did God allow men in Old Testament days to have more than one wife? Please explain the significance of 1 Samuel 1:2

regarding God's seeming favor upon Hannah.

We know from Genesis 2:21-24 that God originally ordained that a man should have one wife. The same principle is stated in Matthew 19:3-6 and Ephesians 5:21-33. But man has always departed from God's standard or ideal. Though polygamy was not pointedly forbidden in the Old Testament, God never condoned it. If you read it, you soon realize that heartache and sorrow was always a result of the practice of polygamy. God did permit it, but He never gave His approval.

The story in 1 Samuel 1 in no way indicates that God is pleased with bigamy. In fact, the cruelty of Peninnah in taunting the childless Hannah illustrates clearly the unhappiness that accompanies all plural marriages. It shows the spirit of rivalry that always appears between women who must share one husband. The Lord blessed Hannah because she was truly a godly woman who poured out her grief to Him in prayer. He answered her petition by giving her a son whom she named Samuel—"heard of God." This incident demonstrates the sad results of bigamy as a violation of the original divine arrangement of one woman for one man, but it also magnifies God's overruling grace.

PRAYER

102.   Please explain the meaning of 1 John 3:22.

And whatever we ask, we receive of Him, because we keep His commandments, and do those things that are pleasing in His sight (1 John 3:22).

This is God's principle governing answered prayer. The entire context of this verse centers upon a believer's confidence toward God because he is walking in obedience to the will of God. Jesus presented this truth clearly when He said, "If ye abide in Me, and My words abide in you, ye shall ask what ye will, and it shall be done unto you" (John 15:7). When the believer is led by the Spirit, is abiding in Christ, and receives His Word into his heart, his prayers will be according to God's will. Obedience to God is a requisite for answered prayer.

103. What about the use of Matthew 18:18,19 in the binding of Satan and the loosing of people from their sins? Is it scriptural to use the formula, "If two of you shall agree on earth as touching anything"?

The misuse of this Scripture has led to many abuses in the practice of prayer. Read the verses over carefully.

> Verily, I say unto you, Whatsoever ye shall bind on earth shall be bound in heaven; and whatsoever ye shall loose on earth shall be loosed in heaven.
> Again I say unto you that if two of you shall agree on earth as touching anything that they shall ask, it shall be done for them by My Father, who is in heaven (Matthew 18:18,19).

Notice first of all that the context of these verses is discipline in the assembly, the church. When you read the entire paragraph, beginning with verse 15 and continuing through verse 20, you see that the church has both a responsibility and an authority.

This passage tells what to do when a fellow believer falls into sin. The Christian is to go first to that sinning brother and tell him his fault personally in the spirit of Galatians 6:1, "Brethren, if a man be overtaken in a fault, ye who are spiritual restore such an one in the spirit of meekness, considering thyself, lest thou also be tempted."

If this rebuke is ignored, then at least two brethren are to speak to him about the matter. If he refuses to listen to them, he is to be brought before the entire assembly. If he will not respond to the church, he is to be excluded from fellowship in that congregation.

It is in this context that we read, "Verily, I say unto you, Whatsoever ye shall bind on earth shall be bound in heaven" (v. 18). A comment by S. Lewis Johnson on this portion is instructive: "If you carry out discipline as set forth here, you can be sure that what you permit on earth is permitted in Heaven, and what you forbid on earth is forbidden in Heaven. In other words, Heaven will follow your actions with Heaven's approval and power . . . . Thus, if the church comes together and action is taken in accordance with Scripture, and discipline is exercised, and if on earth there is an agreement with regard to this thing, it shall be done for them of the Father in Heaven. When the church acts in discipline, this act is carried out by God."

**104.   I have been meditating upon Romans
8:26,27 and feel that true prayer can only
be motivated by the Holy Spirit. Am I right?**

We are told in Ephesians 6:18 that we are to pray with "all prayer and supplication *in the Spirit*." He indwells us and He enables us to pray. He "helpeth our infirmity"; that is, our inability to know the things we should pray for and how to pray. We will never pray in the right way unless the Holy Spirit prays through us. The Christian has both an intercessor above and an intercessor within. Christ is in Heaven pleading *for us* because we are one with Him, and the Holy Spirit is interceding *in us* because we are also one with Him. The longings produced in us by the Spirit are often inexpressible. How wonderful that He intercedes in our behalf with "groanings which cannot be uttered"!

**105.   Would you explain the sentence in the prayer
of Matthew 6 where Jesus taught His
disciples, "Lead us not into temptation"?**

Admittedly, this is a difficult portion. But we can be certain that God would not and cannot lead His children into sin. James wrote, "God cannot be tempted with evil, neither *tempteth He any man*" (James 1:13).

One interpretation of Matthew 6:13 is, "Keep us from temptation." I think, however, that a more suitable treatment can be presented. Remember, this request is followed by the phrase, "but deliver us from evil." Literally, it is "deliver us from *the evil one*." We are to ask that we will not be led into a position where we will be subjected to temptation by Satan.

Every prayer by the believer, of course, must be in accordance with the Lord's will. God is sovereign in His dealing with His children. He knows what is best for each of us, and therefore may expose us to conditions where we might be tempted to evil. If He permits us to come into such a situation, however, we have this assurance: "There hath no temptation taken you but such as is common to man; but God is faithful, who will not permit you to be tempted above that ye are able, but will, with the temptation, also make the way to escape, that ye may be able to bear it" (1 Corinthians 10:13).

When we say, "Lead us not into temptation, but deliver us from evil," we are admitting our human frailty. We recognize the power of Satan and do not trust ourselves. Then, if we are put under a time of testing, we can know that God will strengthen and protect us. He has permitted it to make us stronger Christians.

106. May the Christian rightfully pray "the Lord's prayer," as found in Matthew 6:9-13?

After this manner, therefore, pray ye: Our Father, who art in heaven, Hallowed be Thy name.
Thy kingdom come. Thy will be done in earth, as it is in heaven.
Give us this day our daily bread.
And forgive us our debts, as we forgive our debtors.
And lead us not into temptation, but deliver us from evil. For Thine is the kingdom, and the power, and the glory, forever. Amen (Matthew 6:9-13).

The Lord Jesus gave His disciples this pattern for prayer before the church was formed. A Christian may use a number of the petitions in this prayer without hesitation. Strictly speaking, however, the prayer is part of the Sermon on the Mount—the platform of the kingdom yet to be established on this earth. It will therefore be most applicable to Jewish disciples during the coming tribulation. For the believer today, access to God is available through the name of the Lord Jesus.

You ask, "Is it wrong for me to pray this prayer?" Certainly not! But Christians should understand that the full import of this prayer will be realized in the kingdom age. It was not used in the Acts of the apostles, nor was any direction given in the epistles for its use. Now that the Lord Jesus has ascended, and that the Holy Spirit dwells within the believer and "maketh intercession for us," we may go directly to the Father in the name of the Lord Jesus (see John 16:24).

PREDESTINATION

107. **Please explain John 6:37, "All that the Father giveth Me shall come to Me" in conjunction with John 6:44, "No man can come to Me, except the Father, who hath sent Me, draw him."**

This is a divine truth that is repugnant to the natural man. In our Lord's prayer in John 17 we repeatedly read such words as "...to as many as Thou hast given Him" (v. 2), "...for them whom Thou hast given Me" (v. 9), and "...those whom Thou hast given Me" (v. 11). God has chosen a company of people to be like His Son, and He has given them to Jesus Christ. The apostle Peter spoke of this (see 1 Peter 1:2). Every one of this number will be brought to Jesus Christ in believing faith. Not one of them will be missing.

Because we do not know who will be included in this number, at the command of Christ and in obedience to the Word of God, we plead with all sinners to be reconciled to God. We extend with biblical authority the invitation to "whosoever will." If a person does come to Jesus Christ, it is because the Holy Spirit has given light to his heart. Because of a "drawing" by God, the work of the Spirit has been experienced. Whenever you quote John 1:12, please remember also what verse 13 says, "...not of blood, nor of the will of the flesh, nor of the will of man, *but of God."*

PROMISES

108. Are all of God's promises and covenants conditional?

The word "covenant" means "an agreement" or "contract." It occurs 26 times in the first book of the Bible. Two or more persons are always involved in a covenant. In the scriptural sense, covenants have to do with contractual relationships between God and man. Of course, many of the promises God made in His Word could not be classified as covenants.

Eight covenants are mentioned in the Bible, divided into two classes, conditional and unconditional. A conditional covenant is characterized by the words "if thou wilt." Unconditional covenants are characterized by the phrase, "I will." For your study and consideration, we list the covenants:

Edenic Covenant (Genesis 1:26-2:25).
Adamic Covenant (Genesis 3:14-19).
Noahic Covenant (Genesis 8:20-9:17).
Abrahamic Covenant (Genesis 12:1-4; 13:14-17).
Mosaic Covenant (Exodus 18:8-Exodus 30).
Palestinian Deuteronomic Covenant
(Deuteronomy 30:1-9).
Davidic Covenant (2 Samuel 7:5-19).
The New Covenant (Hebrews 8:6-13;
Matthew 26:26-29).

Of the major covenants, only the Mosiac Covenant is conditional in nature. The fulfillment of its promises was contingent upon Israel's obedience. A helpful footnote in the *New Scofield Reference Edition* of the Bible says, "The human response to the divinely announced purpose is always important, leading as it does to blessing for obedience and discipline for disobedience. But human failure is never permitted to abrogate the covenant or block its ultimate fulfillment." Marvelous fact! All of the covenants meet in the person and work of the Lord Jesus Christ, God's Eternal Word.

PROPHECY

109. **A certain cult claims that the words of Jesus in Luke 10:18, "I beheld Satan as lightning fall from heaven" were fulfilled in 1914. Please explain.**

The claim that this and other prophecies were fulfilled in 1914 is entirely without scriptural basis. Satan does have access to Heaven, as we learn from Revelation 12:10 and Job 1:6-12. Satan is the "god of this age" (2 Corinthians 4:4) and the "prince of the power of the air" (Ephesians 2:2). At present the devil is the ruler of wicked hosts in the heavenlies. In John's vision we see him "cast out into the earth," according to Revelation 12:9. Christ spoke prophetically in Luke 10:18 and in John 12:31, referring to a time that is still future.

PROVISION

110. **What is the meaning of the last part of 2 Corinthians 12:14, "For the children ought not to lay up for the parents, but the parents for the children"?**

When you look at the verses preceding this statement, you note that the apostle was reminding the Corinthian Christians that he had taken no remuneration for his services. He would have had every right to do so, but he had ministered to them without compensation or allowance. He was willing to "spend and be spent" for them (v. 15). As their spiritual father, the apostle Paul was "laying up" for them, rather than asking these spiritual children to take care of him. He wrote, "For though ye have ten thousand instructors in Christ, yet have ye not many fathers; for in Christ Jesus I have begotten you through the gospel" (1 Corinthians 4:15).

RAPTURE

111. Who will be caught up to meet the Lord in the air when He comes?

This question arises because people have heard Bible scholars say that some Christians, if not all, will go through the great tribulation. We are currently experiencing a renaissance of the belief called "post-tribulationism" which takes the position that the saints on earth will not be united to Christ until He returns to establish His kingdom.

I firmly believe, however, the Word of God clearly teaches that every member of Christ's body, the church, will either be translated or resurrected when the Lord Jesus comes to receive all of us unto Himself (1 Thessalonians 4:16,17). First, the dead in Christ will be raised, then living saints will rise to meet Him in the air. We are members of Christ's body entirely by grace. Therefore, no condition of age, walk, service, or growth will preclude our being caught up to meet Him in the air.

The apostle had told the Corinthians that they were carnal. This was evident because of their divisions, envy, strife, factions, immorality, misuse of spiritual gifts, and unworthy partaking of the Lord's supper (see 1 Corinthians 3:3). Yet to these very believers Paul wrote, "We shall not all sleep, but we shall all be changed, in a moment, in the twinkling of an eye, at the last trump" (1 Corinthians 15:51,52).

Chapters 4 and 5 of 1 Thessalonians teach us that *all* believers will be raptured when Christ comes. In fact, 1 Thessalonians declares the Lord's coming *for* His church; 2 Thessalonians depicts His coming *with* His church. It adds that His people will not be on earth in the "day of the Lord" (2 Thessalonians 2:2). Yes, *all* the saved, living and dead, will be caught up to meet the Lord in the air when He comes for His church.

112. Part of your belief about the future is the rapture of the church. If this doctrine is so

important, why did Christ never refer to it in His teaching ministry?

The Lord Jesus did not mention the rapture for a very good reason: the rapture is a *mystery*. In the New Testament sense, a "mystery" was something that had not been previously revealed, but was reserved to be made known at a special time. Christ did not refer to the "catching away" of believers (although He may have implied it in John 14) because it was not to be revealed during His ministry.

The apostle Paul was given the responsibility of making this teaching known. Writing to the Corinthians, he said,

> Behold, I show you a mystery: We shall not all sleep, but we shall all be changed,
> In a moment, in the twinkling of an eye, at the last trump; for the trumpet shall sound, and the dead shall be raised incorruptible, and we shall be changed (1 Corinthians 15:51,52).

God withheld this mystery until after the Lord had died, risen, and ascended on high. In fact, it was not unveiled until after the Holy Spirit had come at Pentecost.

Christ had promised that He had "many things" He wanted His disciples to know, and that the Spirit would reveal them (John 16:12-15). Among them was the truth of the rapture of the church, revealed to Paul by the Holy Spirit and recorded in 1 Thessalonians 4:15-17.

One of the most important mysteries withheld during previous ages but made known through the apostle Paul is the church itself. Shortly after the revelation of this called-out body, made up of all believers in Christ, came the unfolding of the mystery of the Lord Jesus' coming for the saints.

To summarize, the rapture was not mentioned by Christ because it was a mystery. It was to be revealed later by the apostle Paul, who made it known "in due season."

113. Will the church be translated before the identity of Antichrist is known?

Yes, I believe the rapture of the church will precede the revealing of Antichrist, even though it is possible that he could be living today. When the apostle Paul wrote his second epistle to the Thessalonians, the "antichrist philosophy" was already at work. But the identity of Antichrist, the "lawless" one, will not be revealed until "He who now hindereth...be taken out of the way" (2 Thessalonians 2:7). I believe that the hinderer is the Holy Spirit, indwelling the church. It is He who restrains the full manifestation of this evil system. When He is removed, which will occur at the translation of the church, "then shall that wicked one be revealed" (2 Thessalonians 2:8).

REPENTANCE

114. I would like your explanation of repentance. I have been told that I must repent to be saved.

The New Testament word translated "repent," "repentance," or "repented" means "to have another mind" or "to change one's mind." The primary use of the term is demonstrated clearly in Matthew 21:28-31, the parable of the two sons, "...and he came to the first, and said, Son, go work today in my vineyard. He answered and said, I will not; but afterward he repented, and went." In other words, he changed his mind.

In the great salvation gospel written by John, the word "repentance" or "repent" does not appear—yet the word "believe" is used some 100 times. In the book of Romans, given by the Holy Spirit to show how sinners are justified, the word is used only once (Romans 2:4). But repeatedly in the gospels and in Acts, the command is given to repent (Matthew 3:1-3; Luke 13:3,5; Luke 24:25-47; Acts 11:18; Acts 17:29,30).

Why did John not mention repentance in his gospel? Because "believing" on the Lord Jesus Christ includes repentance. Repentance is always connected with faith and is a necessary element of salvation. We are told in 2 Timothy 2:25 that repentance is a gift from God. If it were a work the unbelieving sinner must do to procure God's favor, it would be something man might boast of.

Perhaps the best summation of the one all-inclusive act of repentance and saving faith is to be found in these verses: " . . .how ye turned to God from idols, to serve the living and true God, and to wait for His Son from heaven" (1 Thessalonians 1:9,10). The repentance God requires is a complete change of mind, and is vital in saving faith. The two are one: repentance and faith. They may both be incorporated in the one word "believe."

RESURRECTION

115. Who were the "saints" mentioned in Matthew 27:52,53, who came out of the graves at the time of Jesus' death?

And the graves were opened, and many bodies of the saints that slept were raised,
And came out of the graves after His resurrection, and went into the holy city, and appeared unto many (Matthew 27:52,53).

Notice first of all that their bodies did not come out of the graves when Jesus died, but emerged after the resurrection of Christ (v. 53). Many questions may be asked about this company of saints, but the Bible is strangely silent on the subject. This is the only mention of them. I believe they were part of the "firstfruits" of the resurrection, and were pictured by the sheaf of grain waved before the Lord in celebration of the feast of firstfruits recorded in Leviticus 23. As such, they were not returning to mortal life, but were being translated to another sphere, the eternal. Unlike the raising of Lazerus, the son of the widow of Nain, and the daughter of Jairus (all of whom were restored to mortal life but eventually died again), these saints were given resurrected bodies and immortality.

116. What is meant by "quickening" the mortal body in Romans 8:11?

But if the Spirit of Him that raised up Jesus from the dead dwell in you, He that raised up Christ from the dead shall also give life to your mortal bodies by His Spirit that dwelleth in you (Romans 8:11).

Another translation reads, "But if the Spirit of Him that raised up Jesus from the dead dwell in you, He that raised up Christ from the dead shall also *give life* to your mortal bodies by His Spirit that dwelleth in you." This verse does not refer to any work of the Spirit in our mortal bodies at the present time, but it is speaking of that which will take place at the coming of the Lord Jesus. The "quickening" here is therefore that glorious transformation that will occur to every believer who is alive when the Lord returns to receive us unto Himself. Their bodies will bè instantly changed from mortal to immortal. The "quickening" of those who have died in Christ will be a bit different, for they will be raised from "corruption" to "incorruption."

The quickening of the mortal body, therefore, has no reference to raising a Christian up from sickness. Romans 8:11 looks to the future, and cannot be applied to physical healing today.

117. Second Corinthians 5:1 speaks of a "building of God, . . ."eternal in the heavens." In 1 Corinthians 15 we read of a resurrection body that God will give us. Please reconcile these two statements.

Some Bible teachers say that between death and resurrection, the believer is provided with another body. They identify it as the "building of God, an house not made with hands." Some difficulty is presented in this interpretation, however, by the modifying phrase, "eternal in the heavens." A temporary body could not be called "eternal." I personally believe this is not a reference to a body between death and resurrection, but to the glorified body that will be given the believer when Christ receives His church unto Himself at the first resurrection. When a believer dies, this "earthly house" goes into the grave. But his pure spirit enters directly into the presence of Christ (see 2 Corinthians 5:8). The receiving of the new "house" will take place later at the resurrection of the just. Verses 44 and 49 of 1 Corinthians 15 tell about this new body. The "building of God" refers to the spiritual, eternal body the believer will be given in the future. The assurance of this is expressed by the words "we know" and "we have."

118. What did the apostle Paul mean in Philippians 3:11, "If by any means I might attain unto the resurrection of the dead"?

If we were to examine this verse superficially, we might think Paul was expressing uncertainty about being raised from the dead. A careful look, however, will dispel this idea.

First, observe that in the previous verses Paul had declared his longing to experience more deeply the power of the resurrected Lord. Second, the Greek verb rendered "attain" means "to arrive at" a destination or "to reach" a goal. Therefore, the statement does not imply *earning* the right to be resurrected, but *arriving* at it as a participant.

We must not take the words "if by any means" to indicate uncertainty. An "if" clause is often used when no real doubt is involved. A young married man might say to his wife, "I have willingly given up single life, and will gladly work every day, if only I can come home each evening to you." He is not expressing uncertainty, but only saying this expectation makes his work worthwhile!

Thus, on a higher level, Paul was saying that he would gladly experience the sufferings involved in serving Christ "if only" he could share (as he knew he would) in the first resurrection.

119. Please give me the order of the resurrection mentioned in 1 Corinthians 15:23.

Our Lord states clearly in John 5:29 that there are two resurrections: one to life and one to damnation. The resurrection of life is in several stages, just as the typical harvest feast in Leviticus 23 includes three phases: (1) the wave sheaf of firstfruits; (2) the main harvest; (3) the gleanings. This is the order: Christ was the firstfruits (1 Corinthians 15:23); the resurrection of believers in the rapture of the church is the main harvest (1 Thessalonians 4:16); and the resurrection of tribulation saints and Old Testament believers at the second coming of our Lord Jesus is the gleanings (Revelation 20:3,4; Daniel 12:2). The second resurrection—that "to damnation"—occurs at the end of the millennium (Revelation 20:5,12,14).

REVERENCE

120. How should God be addressed? I was always taught that to speak to Him as "You" showed irreverence, and that Jesus always addressed God as "Thee" and "Thou." Does the original Greek make a distinction?

The form of the pronoun used in addressing God is a matter of individual choice. Reverence or irreverence is determined by the attitude of the heart. "The sacrifices of God are a broken spirit; a broken and a contrite heart, O God, Thou wilt not despise" (Psalm 51:17). "Thee" and "Thou" are forms of the pronoun used in the 17th century, when the *King James Version* was translated. Many of us use only these forms in praying to God, primarily because we have done so from early childhood. Personally, I prefer it. But many Christians address God reverently as "You." There is no distinction made in the Greek language that would indicate the mandatory use of "Thee" and "Thou." Whichever you decide to use, I would advise consistency. To borrow a sentence from Romans 14:5, "Let every man be fully persuaded in his own mind."

REWARDS

121. Please explain Matthew 20:16, "Many are called, but few chosen."

These same words occur at the end of chapter 19 in response to the disciples' question, "What shall we have, therefore?" (Matthew 19:27). Our Lord is teaching about the rewards of the kingdom. Remember, a parable is used to demonstrate a principle. Therefore, if we seek to assign a specific meaning to every little thing mentioned, we soon run into trouble.

We are so quickly taken up with the matter of rewards that we forget that all we have or ever will have, all we are or ever will be, must be credited to the grace of God. The principle our Lord was emphasizing here is simply that God is sovereign, and that He will give rewards as it pleases Him. Salvation certainly is not in view—but rewards. Our sovereign Lord will thereby magnify His grace.

122. What is the explanation of 1 Corinthians 9:27? Was the apostle Paul afraid of losing his salvation? If not, then what was he referring to in this verse?

But I keep under my body, and bring it into subjection, lest that by any means, when I have preached to others, I myself should be a castaway (1 Corinthians 9:27).

Allow me to answer the second question first. Absolutely not! When Paul said, "...lest that by any means...I myself should be a castaway," he was *not* referring to salvation at all. Rather, he was talking about rewards for service. It helps us to keep in mind that the picture he was using in this portion of 1 Corinthians is that of the athlete. In particular, he was making reference to the running games that were so popular throughout the Roman Empire at that time. A person who participates in a race must abide by the regulations or be disqualified. In addition, if he hopes to win, he must train thoroughly, subduing his body and bringing it under his control. If he does not, he will be "disapproved" or "set aside."

The apostle was using this image to speak of his own ministry. If he were to become proud, insistent upon his rights, or careless about the flesh, he would miss the reward. Paul did not want to be "shelved" here. Nor did he want to have his service disapproved at the *bema*, the judgment seat of Christ.

RUTH

123. **How do you reconcile the fact that Ruth the Moabitess entered the "congregation of the Lord" when Deuteronomy 23:3 declares that a Moabite should not enter?**

Let me begin by saying that the laws of Deuteronomy 23 are restricted to men, for only males could enter "the congregation of the Lord." We must remember, of course, that this had to do with civil and ceremonial rights and privileges, not with salvation. Many distinctions were maintained under the Mosaic system, some involving Gentile women who had married men of Israel (see Nehemiah 13:1-3). But personal faith brought salvation to every believer then, just as now.

Second, the marriage of Boaz to Ruth was valid because she had been converted to faith in Israel's God. The Lord strongly forbade intermarriage with the heathen, but Ruth no longer could be classified among those who worshiped false gods because of her belief in Jehovah.

Third, Jewish law declared that all legal rights came through the father. The Moabite ancestry of Ruth, therefore, was no handicap to her children.

SAINTS

124. Does the word "saints" in the Bible always refer to the church age (Zechariah 14:5; 1 Thessalonians 3:13; Revelation 20:9)?

Since the Bible uses the word "saint" to refer to the godly in general, we must always note the context when it appears. The term is used in both the Old and New Testaments to mean that which is "sanctified" or "set apart to God." Ordinarily, when the Old Testament refers to "saints," the church is not in view—only the godly of Israel. The prophecy of Daniel 7:18 may include the saints of the church age, however, because they will reign with Christ 1,000 years. Again, the context must be carefully considered.

The word for "saints" as used in the New Testament does not signify someone who has achieved a superior level of spiritual attainment. Every believer is a saint because of his standing or position *in Christ*.

SALVATION

125. I know that salvation is by grace and not by works. However, will you explain what the Bible means when it says in Philippians 2:12, "...work out your own salvation with fear and trembling"?

If you will identify the people whom Paul was addressing, you will learn that they were "the saints in Christ Jesus" (Philippians 1:1). These people were believers; they were saved. So, it was not necessary for them to work for a salvation they already possessed.

Furthermore, to interpret this verse to mean that we must work for our salvation would be contrary to all other scriptural teaching. Consider, for instance, several very familiar verses. Ephesians 2:8,9 states, "For by grace are ye saved through faith; and that not of yourselves, it is the *gift* of God—not of works, lest any man should boast." Titus 3:5 says, "Not by *works* of righteousness which we

have done, but according to His mercy He saved us ...."
Romans 6:23 declares, "...the *gift* of God is eternal life
through Jesus Christ, our Lord."

A key to the meaning of Philippians 2:12 is found in
the verb translated "work out." This word means "to carry
out to the goal, to carry to its ultimate conclusion."

Let me illustrate what this expression "work out"
means. Mathematics was not my best subject in school.
Many an assignment involved long hours as I struggled to
complete the problems given for homework. The purpose
of those assignments was to "work out"—to carry to an
ultimate goal or conclusion—each mathematical
problem. The apostle was saying in essence to those
Christians at Philippi, "Work it out; carry it out to the
goal. Yours is a salvation not only from sin's penalty but
also from sin's power in your life. Don't stop short."

The believer already has salvation. But he also has the
responsibility to live a Christian life. We are to carry out
our salvation to this ultimate goal or conclusion. What is
ours *within* is to be evidenced *without*.

The salvation given to us, apart from any work that we
might do, is now to be "worked out" in us. But how is this
done? Verse 13 has the answer. Verse 12 gives the
responsibility; verse 13 is the divine enablement: "For it
is God who worketh in you both to will and to do of His
good pleasure." Speaking of the Holy Spirit, the Lord
Jesus said, "He dwelleth with you, and shall be in you"
(John 14:17). When we yield our wills to the Holy Spirit,
He makes us willing to "work out" this salvation. He not
only gives the *desire* to be like Christ, but He also gives
the *power* "both to *will* and *to do* of His good pleasure."

God's commands carry with them God's enabling. The
grace of God that brings us salvation also teaches "us
that, denying ungodliness and worldly lusts, we should
live soberly, righteously, and godly, in this present age"
(Titus 2:12). This is what it means to "work out your own
salvation."

126. **Please explain 1 Timothy 4:16. Since the epistles were written to Christians, does this justify the belief that saved people can be lost?**

The verse concludes with the words, "... for in doing this thou shalt both save thyself and them that hear thee." This "salvation" has nothing to do with eternal life or the saving of the soul. Paul was admonishing Timothy to pay close attention to the doctrine, telling him to "give attendance to reading, to exhortation, to doctrine" (v. 13). By doing this, he would be protected from error, and those who heard him would be delivered as well.

Eternal salvation is not in view here at all. The word "save" in this verse carried the principal idea of "deliverance or protection," and is used in the same sense in Philippians 2:12. The "deliverance" is from the dangers of false doctrine.

127. **I find Matthew 7:21-23 confusing. Would you explain these verses for me?**

Not every one that saith unto Me, Lord, Lord,
shall enter into the kingdom of heaven, but he that
doeth the will of My Father, who is in heaven.
Many will say to Me in that day, Lord, Lord,
have we not prophesied in Thy name? And in Thy
name have cast out demons? And in Thy name done
many wonderful works?
And then will I profess unto them, I never
knew you; depart from Me, ye that work iniquity
(Matthew 7:21-23).

The judgment to be pronounced by Christ upon those who stand before Him, calling Him "Lord, Lord," indicates that they have not believed on Him. It's a case of profession of faith without genuine possession of life in Christ. Not only will they be unmasked by phonies, but they will also be shown to have performed miracles under some power other than Christ's name. In other words, in this age some will prophesy, cast out demons, or do wonderful works by the power of Satan. Do not forget: the devil is a master counterfeiter. But to these wicked impostors Christ will say, "I never knew you; depart from Me, ye that work iniquity or [lawlessness]."

The specific time that our Lord will enact this judgment is at His return to establish His kingdom upon this earth. When He comes, some who had performed many works and had used His name will turn out to be mere professors of Christ and not true believers.

128. Please explain 2 Peter 2:20-22. Is it possible for someone to escape the pollution of the world and still not be saved?

Yes, I believe this is possible. Verse 22 gives the answer. "The dog is turned to his own vomit again; and the sow that was washed, to her wallowing in the mire." But the Scripture never calls a true believer a dog or a sow. Peter wrote, "But it is happened unto *them*...." This is the case of some people who had reformed outwardly, but whose hearts had never experienced a work of regeneration. Those who are truly born again will not turn away from "the holy commandment delivered unto them" (2 Peter 2:21). Read the entire chapter to get the full description of these "false teachers," and you will readily see that the apostle is not describing true believers in Christ.

129. What provision is made for infants and children who die before reaching the age of accountability?

Quite often at the funeral of a child you will hear the minister read, "And He took them up in His arms, put His hands upon them, and blessed them" (Mark 10:16). But this passage gives no assurance of life after death for these children, nor does it bestow the blessedness of the saved.

The first seven chapters of Leviticus record the seven offerings that typify the person and work of Christ, both Godward and manward. Two of these are the trespass offering and the sin offering. Christ was both the offering for *what we are* by nature—sinners; and *what we do* as the result of this nature—sins or trespasses.

Is an infant or a child, though unaccountable, a sinner by nature? Most certainly, for he was born with a sinful nature (Psalm 51:5). Christ became the "sin offering" for that one (read 2 Corinthians 5:21). Children are therefore fully covered by the offering of our Lord at Calvary.

If a child reaches the age when he is accountable for "sins" and recognizes good from evil, he must make a personal decision to accept the sacrifice of our Lord, "Who His own self bore our sins in His own body on the tree" (1 Peter 2:24).

130. What was the basis for Old Testament salvation? Were there Christians before Christ came to earth?

No one can be a Christian without Christ. The term "Christian" is first mentioned in Acts 11:26 in connection with the believers at Antioch. But how were the Old Testament saints declared righteous before God? We are told plainly in Hebrews 10:4 that "it is not possible that the blood of bulls and of goats should take away sins."

Salvation has always been a gift from God received by faith. Those of Old Testament times were saved by faith in a *coming* Redeemer. We are saved by faith in One who *has come*. The prime Old Testament example is Abraham. "For what saith the Scripture? Abraham believed God, and it was counted unto him for righteousness" (Romans 4:3). God imputes righteousness to the one who believes, who places his faith in the promise of God. Here is the clincher! "But to him that worketh not, but believeth on Him that justifieth the ungodly, his faith is counted for righteousness" (Romans 4:5). Faith in the promised Redeemer is what credited God's righteousness to the account of the believing Old Testament sinner.

131. Will those who have heard the gospel but have not received the Lord Jesus be given any opportunity to be saved during the tribulation?

I am convinced that people who have deliberately and defiantly rejected the Lord Jesus in this age of grace will *not* turn to Him during the great tribulation. Paul indicated this very clearly in 2 Thessalonians 2:9-12, where he said that God will send these Christ-rejecters "strong delusion, that they should believe the lie." Large numbers certainly will be saved during the tribulation period, after the church is raptured. Revelation 7:9 portrays them as "a great multitude, which no man could number." But none will be included who previously had been confronted with the claims of Christ and turned away in unbelief to continue in their own sinful ways.

SATAN

132. **Please explain 2 Samuel 24. In verse 1 we are told that the Lord's anger was kindled against Israel, and that He incited David to number the people. Then, in verse 10, David repented and confessed that he had sinned when he did so. Would God cause us to do that which is wrong?**

The Lord would never cause any man to do wrong! The apostle James wrote, "Let no man say when he is tempted, I am tempted of God; for God cannot be tempted with evil, neither tempteth He any man" (James 1:13).

The Septuagint (Greek) version of the Old Testament gives us help in understanding this passage about David. It translates 2 Samuel 24:1, " . . .and Satan moved David" rather than, " . . and He [God] incited David." When we read 1 Chronicles 21:l, we can readily see that this is the preferred translation. This verse states very definitely that "Satan stood up against Israel, and enticed David."

Of this you can be sure: Satan could only go as far as God permitted him. When you read the entire account, you discover that great prosperity had caused David and the people to be filled with pride. They took all the glory to themselves rather than honoring the Lord. This gave Satan an opportunity to hinder David, and it also called for God's chastening. The corrective action did come from the hand of the Lord, "For whom the Lord loveth He chasteneth" (Hebrews 12:6).

133. Does Revelation 12:10 indicate that Satan has access to Heaven?

Yes, it does. In addition to the reference in Revelation 12:10, we have the account in Job 1:6-12 where Satan or Lucifer appeared before the Lord with the "sons of God" (undoubtedly created angelic beings) and made charges against Job. Today he is still the "accuser of the brethren," and he will continue to have access to God's presence until the time of his "casting down," depicted in Revelation 12:7-12. I believe this will occur at the beginning of the great tribulation. The Lord Jesus spoke prophetically of this "casting out" in Luke 10:18.

This does not mean, however, that the devil can enter the third heaven, spoken of by God in Isaiah 57:15. The Lord says here that He dwells in "the high and holy place," the paradise to which Paul referred in 2 Corinthians 12:1-5. It was from this realm, where no sin can enter, that Satan was deposed when he first rebelled (see Isaiah 14:12). The devil is now the "prince of the power of the air" (Ephesians 2:2), a superterrestrial region where he and his fallen followers engage in an invisible warfare with the holy angels. This heavenly area is where Satan appears before God to accuse us, and from which he directs his operations on earth. The Revelation 12 passage portrays his banishment from this region.

134. Do the terms "Lucifer" in Isaiah 14:12 and "the anointed cherub" in Ezekiel 28:13,14 refer specifically to Satan?

Isaiah 14 can be understood only when we recognize it as a poetic passage in the form of a song. It taunts the fallen king of Babylon and expresses Israel's final triumph. In colorful and awesome imagery, it portrays the Babylonian tyrant entering sheol, the place of the dead. The inhabitants are sufficiently conscious to wonder at the fall of such a mighty one. They marvel that he, like themselves, has been brought low in death. A mighty man who on earth had perpetrated devastation and death was finally to make his abode among the eternally lost ones.

In their prophetic perspective, these verses in Isaiah 14 point to Antichrist. Like all the Babylonian kings, he is looked upon as a representative of Satan. The pride and ambition expressed in verses 13 and 14, and the name "Lucifer" which means "the brilliant one," can be attributed only to the devil.

Ezekiel 28 also addresses an earthly king, the prince of Tyre. But here, also, the language obviously looks beyond this realm to Satan himself. In verses 12 through 15 he is described as having once been a sinless, angelic being, but now he is fallen because of rebellion.

In both Isaiah 14 and Ezekiel 28, therefore, the prophets have immediate reference to an earthly king, but their words ultimately point beyond. They describe Satan, that once-exalted creature who was cast out of Heaven because of sin and is now the archenemy of God and His people.

135. Would you please explain Genesis 3:15? I don't understand it.

This remarkable prophecy is actually the first promise in the Bible of the coming Redeemer. It predicts the opposition He would encounter and the outcome. The verse reads,

> And I will put enmity between thee and the woman,
> and between thy seed and her seed; He shall bruise
> thy head, and thou shalt bruise His heel (Genesis
> 3:15).

These words were spoken by God to Satan. The conflict and conquest they describe may be outlined as follows:
1. The prediction of enmity between Satan and the woman.
2. Enmity between the seed of the serpent and the seed of the woman foretold.
3. The prophecy of the bruising of the Savior's heel and the serpent's head.

The first part of this announcement speaks of the continuing antagonism between Satan and the woman. Some Bible scholars say this points to Eve's repentance for her sin and her continuing hostility toward Satan, who caused her to sin. Others follow the metaphorical description of Revelation 12 and identify the woman as Israel.

The second part speaks of the two "seeds." The seed of

the serpent is Antichrist; the seed of the woman is Christ. More than this, He is the "seed of the woman" in that He was born of a virgin. He was *not* the seed of man, which means that He was not implicated in the sin of Adam. Spotlessly born, He could be our Redeemer. The ultimate confrontation between God and Satan will be focused in the conflict between Christ and Antichrist.

Part three is the twofold prophecy of "bruising." The heel of the Redeemer was bruised at Calvary, where He suffered for our sin and died to pay its penalty. The head of the serpent will be "bruised" by Christ at His glorious return. Paul wrote, "And the God of peace shall bruise Satan under your feet shortly" (Romans 16:20).

SELAH

136. What does "selah" mean?

This word appears about 70 times in the Psalms and the book of Habakkuk. Its meaning is uncertain. It is derived from one of two Hebrew words, one meaning "to lift up" and the other "to pause." It may have been a musical sign for the temple singers and musicians. Like "amen" and "hallelujah," it most likely was an indication for the worshiper to reflect upon the solemn truth expressed. The psalmists used it in different settings. Sometimes after they stated rather disturbing facts as in Psalm 140:3, "selah" was used for encouragement—as if they were saying, "Lift up your heart to God." On other occasions it appears to be an expression of wonder, as noted in Psalm 46:7,11. For the reader today, it is a signal that the Lord has just made or is about to make a significant statement.

SECOND COMING

137. Is the "last trumpet" of Revelation 11 identical with the "last trump" of 1 Corinthians 15:52?

I do not believe it is necessary to make these two events identical. The word "last" can signify two different things:

it may be last in point of time, or it may be the final time or event in a series. The trumpets of Revelation 11 and Matthew 24 refer primarily to Israel, but the "last trump" of 1 Corinthians 15:52 and the trump of 1 Thessalonians 4 will be for the church. Very possibly, the program of God for both the church and for Israel may be ended by the blowing of a trumpet. In either case, therefore, it would be the "last" trump.

SHEEP OF CHRIST'S FLOCK

138. In John 10:16 Jesus said, "And other sheep I have, that are not of this fold; them also I must bring, and they shall not hear My voice; and there shall be one fold, and one shepherd." Who are the other sheep? What is this "fold"?

This verse appears in the familiar passage where Christ identified Himself as the Good Shepherd. You will observe by reading the context that the sheep our Lord first mentioned as being in the fold are the Jews. This nation had been the special, chosen flock of God, ordained to receive His revelation, to obey Him in sacrifices and in life, and to be a witness to the world. God's redemptive activity had centered in Israel.

But now things would change. The Jews were to reject their Messiah and crucify Him. God would now shift His redemptive activity to another flock. The "other sheep" Jesus referred to here are the Gentiles. Christ was making it known that all mankind would now share in the offer of salvation.

You see, the glorious truth of Ephesians 3:1-6, that Gentiles would be fellow heirs with Christ, members of the same body and partakers of God's promise in Christ by the gospel, had not yet been made known. In John 10:16, therefore, our Lord was giving a hint of what would come to pass after His death and resurrection. The offer of salvation would be made to all, and millions who were not Jews would be saved and enter God's family as inheritors of the kingdom. Gentile sheep would be gathered. Along with

saved Jews, they would compose the church, the body of
Christ. Although the verse reads, "...and there shall be
one fold," it would be better rendered, "...there shall be
one flock." When Jesus spoke these words, He was looking forward to the church, made up of both saved Jews
and saved Gentiles.

SHEKINAH

**139. Please explain what you mean by the
"shekinah." You used this expression on
your program, and I cannot find it anywhere
in the Bible.**

You have asked a good question that has apparently
bothered others as well. First of all, you are correct in
observing that this term does not appear anywhere in the
Bible. The word "shekinah" is the transliteration of a
Hebrew word that means "to dwell" or "to reside."

Second, the Old Testament Scripture contains many
allusions to God "abiding with" or "dwelling with" men.
You will recall that a cloud rested over the ark of the covenant in the most holy place of the tabernacle. When it was
there, "the glory of the Lord filled the tabernacle" (Exodus
40:34). God dwelt in the midst of the people of Israel, and
His presence was reflected in the glory-cloud.

A similar expression is found in Ezekiel 43, where the
prophet was given a vision of "the glory of the God of
Israel" (Ezekiel 43:2). Here is the prophet's description:

> Afterward, he brought me to the gate, even the gate
> that looketh toward the east,
> And, behold, the glory of the God of Israel came
> from the way of the east; and His voice was like a
> noise of many waters, and the earth shined with His
> glory.
> And it was according to the appearance of the
> vision which I saw, even according to the vision that I
> saw when I came to destroy the city; and the visions
> were like the vision that I saw by the river, Chebar;
> and I fell upon my face.

And the glory of the Lord came into the house by the way of the gate whose prospect is toward the east.

So the Spirit took me up, and brought me into the inner court, and, behold, the glory of the Lord filled the house (Ezekiel 43:1-5).

Verse 4 tells us that the glory of the Lord entered the house from a gate that looked eastward. This was evidently a physical manifestation—something the people could see. It was the *shekinah*, the "glory cloud" which indicated to the people that God was dwelling with them. This is precisely what we have in mind when we speak of the "shekinah glory."

SIN

140. Please explain Genesis 3:17, "Cursed is the ground for thy sake," and Genesis 8:21, "I will not again curse the ground anymore for man's sake."

The first of these declarations of God was given following the sin of Adam; the second came when Noah built an altar to the Lord after the flood. They do not represent a reversal of God's judgment; neither do they contradict each other.

You will note the words in the second, "I will not *again* curse the ground *anymore*." God was simply saying here that He would never place another curse upon the ground. Note that at the same time He also said, "Neither will I again smite anymore everything living, as I have done" (Genesis 8:21).

The Lord was not abrogating judgment. Rather, in this promise that He would never again destroy the race with a flood, He was displaying His *grace*.

141. In view of Matthew 6:14,15, if a person is persistently unforgiving, does that mean he is not forgiven by God? Or has he never been born again?

> For if ye forgive men their trespasses, your heavenly Father will also forgive you;
> But if ye forgive not men their trespasses, neither will your Father forgive your trespasses (Matthew 6:14,15).

No, I do not believe these verses teach that an unforgiving Christian is not forgiven by God, or that he loses his salvation. However, if we do not practice a spirit of love and forgiveness toward those who have wronged us, certainly we will not be able to enjoy full communion with the Heavenly Father. The norm for the believer is stated clearly in Ephesians 4:32, "And be ye kind one to another, tenderhearted, forgiving one another, even as God, for Christ's sake, hath forgiven you." An unforgiving spirit breaks fellowship with God and keeps our prayers from being answered.

142. For if we sin willfully after we have received the knowledge of the truth, there remaineth no more sacrifice for sins (Hebrews 10:26).

No, this is not a case of denied forgiveness. Rather, it says that if the believer refuses to take advantage of the intercessory work of the Lord Jesus Christ by confessing and forsaking his sin, he can expect God to chasten him. The context of the entire passage makes this clear.

Please note the occurrence of the personal pronoun "we," and that the object of the writer's admonition in verse 19 is "brethren." Then observe that verse 26 begins, "For if *we*," indicating that it was addressed to true believers. The Word of God is positively clear that no Christian can fall away and be lost (John 10:28,29). Therefore, something else must be in view in this passage. I believe it is a case of willful, continuing, presumptuous sin, or as it is called in John's epistle, "sin unto death" (1 John 5:16). Verse 27 indicates that the chastening of the Lord will fall upon such a Christian, and verse 30 states, "The Lord shall judge His people." This may even be in the form of physical death, such as Ananias and Sapphira (Acts 5). Most certainly it applies to the judgment seat of Christ, which will be a "fiery indignation" for some because they were "saved, yet as by fire" (1 Corinthians 3:15).

143. Please explain Psalm 19:13 where David prayed to be kept from "presumptuous sin." If one should sin in this manner, can he be forgiven for it?

The law on presumptuous sin is stated in Numbers 15:30,31. If an Israelite or a stranger in the land sinned in this way, the law required that his soul "be cut off from among his people." What was this sin? Specifically, it was "despising the word of the Lord." It was deliberately going against what God had plainly commanded. The penalty prescribed by the law was death. David did not want to sin presumptuously and be judged with death as a consequence. In this day of grace, the promise of 1 John 1:9 is, "If we confess our sins, He is faithful and just to forgive us our sins, and to cleanse us from all unrighteousness." This provision is precious indeed.

But let me warn you. It *is* possible for a Christian to commit a "sin unto death" (1 John 5:16). This could be compared to the "presumptuous sin"—deliberately going against God's revealed will in His Word. The committing of the deed, along with an unwillingness to confess and forsake the sin, may result in God's chastening by physical death. Therefore, every Christian should be sensitive to the direction of the Word and the leading of the indwelling Holy Spirit.

SINLESS PERFECTION

144. How do you harmonize 2 Corinthians 5:17 and 1 John 3:6,8,9 with 1 John 1:8? If a Christian is a "new creation" and "doth not

commit sin," why does the Bible tell us, "If
we say that we have no sin, we deceive
ourselves, and the truth is not in us"?

The difficulties in finding conformity between these
verses lies with two statements in the 1 John 3 passage:
"Whosoever abideth in Him sinneth not" (v. 6) and
"Whosoever is born of God doth not commit sin" (v. 9).
They make it sound as if a believer never sins.

But the answer is to be found in an accurate translation
of the Greek words translated "sinneth not" and "doth not
commit sin" (1 John 3:6,9). They are both in the present
tense, which implies habit, practice, or unbroken
sequence. Neither verse, therefore, is speaking of a single
act of sin, but rather of a pattern of life. The terms used in
verses 6 and 9 are equivalent to the verb "practice."

That the believer does sin is stated clearly in 1 John
1:8,10; 2:l. The apostle is quick to admit this and to
prescribe the remedy. "If we confess our sins, He is faithful and just to forgive us our sins, and to cleanse us from
all unrighteousness" (1 John 1:9). But the believer does
not "practice" sin; it is no longer the ruling principle of his
life. The unregenerate sinner continues in his sin; it is the
habit of his life.

The new nature—that which is born of God at salvation—cannot sin, for it is God's nature. The person who
has this new nature within does not "practice" sin. It's no
longer his habitual way of life. George Williams in "Student's Commentary on the Holy Scriptures" put it this
way: "Sin dwells and reigns in man; it dwells but does not
reign in the believer. His heart, like the magnetic needle,
may be disturbed by a temporary attraction, but it hastens
to its resting-point, to which it always returns. Whoever is
truly born of God does not live a life of sinning."

**145.   I keep falling back into old habits. With the
blessed Holy Spirit living within, isn't it
possible for us to live without sin? Isn't the
old nature supposed to be gone?**

The Holy Spirit dwells within the believer, not to sanction
what is produced by the old nature, but as the seal of what

is of Christ, the new nature. Never for one moment are we to excuse any evil within ourselves. We are to judge it, and everything that is inconsistent with God's holiness is to be put away. The indwelling Spirit demands the judgment of evil in every shape and form.

Having acknowledged this, we must also recognize what the Word of God teaches about the old nature. It is not eradicated when we are saved; nor is it transformed. It remains the same, and it can only produce fruit after its own kind—evil. Christ said to Nicodemus, "That which is born of the flesh is flesh."

The apostle John realistically faced this when he wrote, "If we say that we have no sin, we deceive ourselves, and the truth is not in us" (1 John 1:8). John recognized indwelling sin. He spoke not only of the believer still possessing the old nature but also of the fruit of that nature—sin. "If we say that we have not sinned, we make Him a liar, and His word is not in us" (1 John 1:10).

As the believer grows in the knowledge that he is identified with Christ in His death and resurrection, and as he reckons himself "to be dead indeed unto sin, but alive unto God through Jesus Christ" (Romans 6:11), he will begin to experience a moment-by-moment victory over sin. He will have an abiding fellowship with the Lord. But when he breaks that fellowship by sin, the child of God will quickly restore it by following the admonition of 1 John 1:9, "If we confess our sins, He is faithful and just to forgive us our sins, and to cleanse us from all unrighteousness."

Because the old nature is not removed when we are regenerated, we must still battle the world, the flesh, and the devil. At times we will fall, but as we grow in Christ and yield to the indwelling Holy Spirit we'll become stronger and stronger. When we do sin, we can follow the avenue of confession and forgiveness and be restored to fellowship with God.

SOUL AND SPIRIT

146. Is man of a triune nature—body, soul, and spirit? Or are the soul and spirit the same?

We often do use the words "soul" and "spirit" interchangeably. The Bible, however, distinguishes clearly between the two. In 1 Thessalonians 5:23, Paul wrote, "I pray God your whole spirit and soul and body be preserved blameless unto the coming of our Lord Jesus Christ." I believe that in Hebrews 4:12 the writer indicates that soul and spirit can be separated or divided, " ...piercing even to the dividing asunder of soul and spirit...."

The "spirit" of man is that part which is capable of God-consciousness. The "soul" is that which makes man self-conscious, having affections, emotions, desires, and will. But even the spirit of man, unrenewed through the new birth, cannot know the things of God unless the Holy Spirit reveals them (see 1 Corinthians 2:11-15). In Proverbs 20:27 we read that "The spirit of man is the lamp of the Lord [or the candle of Jehovah], searching all the inward parts." When a man is saved, born again, this "candle" is set aflame. It is then that "the Spirit Himself beareth witness with our spirit, that we are the children of God" (Romans 8:16).

Furthermore, two entirely different words are used in the New Testament for soul and spirit. The Greek word for soul is *psuche*, while the word used for spirit is *pneuma*. The Bible therefore does distinguish between soul and spirit.

SPIRIT

147. In 1 Corinthians 12:10, as Paul was speaking about the different gifts, he mentioned the "discerning of spirits." I would like your comment on that.

One of the *harismata*, the gifts of the Spirit bestowed on believers, was the ability to discern the spirits. This was not the power to see into the minds of men; but rather, knowing how to evaluate correctly the work of spiritual beings. The apostle John commanded, "Beloved, believe not every spirit, but test the spirits whether they are of God" (1 John 4:1). I personally believe that the particular gift mentioned here was the ability to determine the source of revelation—whether it came from God or Satan. Remember, the inspired Word was not yet written as we have it today in the New Testament. Anyone claiming to receive a prophecy or revelation from Heaven today that goes beyond what is already written in the Bible is not speaking by the Holy Spirit.

148. Please explain 1 Samuel 18:10. Can an evil spirit come from God?

> And it came to pass on the next day, that the evil spirit from God came upon Saul, and he prophesied in the midst of the house; and David played with his hand, as at other times; and there was a javelin in Saul's hand (1 Samuel 18:10).

I firmly believe that an evil spirit never comes directly from God. But I am also convinced that neither Satan nor his cohorts are able to do anything unless God permits it. An example of this is found in the story of Job. God allowed the devil to afflict and test the patriarch, but set limits which the evil one could not go beyond.

The Hebrew writers realized that God is in ultimate control, even though He permitted wicked creatures to do their work. Therefore, they sometimes attributed the evil to God. For that reason, when we read in 1 Samuel 18:10 that an "evil spirit from God came upon Saul," we must not infer that it was sent from the Lord. He merely allowed it. God can never be the author of evil.

TIMES OF THE GENTILES

149. Kindly give an explanation of the terms "the times of the Gentiles" (Luke 21:24) and "the fullness of the Gentiles" (Romans

11:25). Are they the same? When do they occur?

Perhaps the best way to answer these questions is to consider each text separately. This will enable you to compare and contrast what the Bible teaches about these phrases.

The times of the Gentiles is the period of history that began when God gave universal authority to Nebuchadnezzar. The image of Daniel 2 describes the entire era. Four great world powers are included: Babylon (the head of gold), Medo-Persia (the chest and arms of silver), Greece (the torso and thighs of bronze), and Rome (the legs and feet of iron and clay).

Each of these empires defeated Jerusalem and established worldwide authority. The last of them, Rome, will appear again in revived form. Its ruler will be Antichrist, the man of sin, who will set out to conquer Jerusalem once again and reign over the world. But that kingdom will be destroyed, as is pictured by the smiting stone of Daniel 2. This "stone" from the mountain that smote the image is a picture of the Lord Jesus Christ, who will come again as King of kings and Lord of lords to overthrow the restored Roman Empire and defeat Antichrist. When He does, the "times of the Gentiles" will be at an end. Christ will then establish His kingdom of peace and righteousness, and He will reign over the entire earth.

The fullness of the Gentiles is a reference to the people God is calling out from among the nations (the Gentiles) during the present dispensation of grace. After Christ was rejected by the Jews, God's redemptive activity shifted from Israel to the Gentiles. Salvation is now offered to everyone by faith in the Lord Jesus. The Bible tells us that God is taking out from among the nations "a people for His name" (Acts 15:14). These "called out" ones are formed into the church. When the last member is added to this body, the last stone fitted into this building, the church will be complete and the "fullness of the Gentiles" will have come.

God will then turn His attention once again to Israel. All the promises of the Old Testament concerning that nation will be fulfilled, "and so all Israel shall be saved." In Romans 11:26 and 27, the Bible tells us how that will take place.

These two phrases therefore describe two completely different subjects. The "times of the Gentiles" speaks of the political domination of the world by four great world powers; the "fullness of the Gentiles" depicts that day when the church, the body of Christ, is complete, and the focus of redemptive history shifts once again to Israel.

TRIBULATION

150.   Joel 2:1-10 speaks of terrible destruction, terror, and death. What is the prophet referring to in this passage?

In his first chapter, Joel wrote about a devastating plague of locusts. He was illustrating the plight of Israel and Palestine in the "times of the Gentiles." He described wave after wave of insects sweeping through the land and devouring everything in their path. In like manner, the land of Israel has become the prey of the succeeding Gentiles powers. This accurately depicts the history of the Jews.

In chapter 2, however, Joel has another time in view. His vision was announced by the words, "Let all the inhabitants of the land tremble; for the day of the Lord cometh, for it is near at hand" (Joel 2:1). Verses 2 through 10 undoubtedly refer to the hordes of Assyrians who would invade Israel from the north like a plague of locusts. But they also have a further application: because they refer to the "day of the Lord," they no doubt picture a still future invasion of Palestine.

In the endtime, Israel will again be threatened by a foe whose armies will march down from the north (v. 20). Their intent will be to destroy the people of God and devastate their land. They will come just before the glorious appearing of the Lord Jesus Christ to establish His kingdom on the earth.

The prophets often predicted events that would have a double fulfillment—one in the immediate future, and another in the endtimes. This is one more example of a prophecy with a dual fulfillment.

151. We would like an explanation of Matthew 24:22. Does this mean that the 144,000 will be in hiding for the last half of the tribulation?

And except those days should be shortened, there should no flesh be saved; but for the elect's sake, those days shall be shortened (Matthew 24:22).

This verse is part of a passage that deals exclusively with the last half of Daniel's seventieth week, the great tribulation (Daniel 9:27). This is "the time of Jacob's trouble" and the context clearly indicates that Christ is talking about Israel. Now I agree that in the corporate sense the "elect" can either refer to the nation of Israel or to the church (Isaiah 45:4; Ephesians 1:4). Interpreting this verse from the context, however, I would positively identify these men as "the elect" of Israel who have the seal of God in their foreheads (see Revelation 7:4-8). The outpouring of terrible judgment will be withheld from the earth until these 144,000 are in a place of safety.

152. When will those who believe on Christ during the tribulation ever come before Him in judgment of their works?

I find no conclusive answer to this question in the Bible. We read in Revelation 7:9-17 that a "great multitude" from all nations will be saved during the tribulation. Most of these will experience martyrdom, for a great host of them are seen before the throne of God. They will have been born again as a result of hearing the gospel proclaimed by the sealed remnant out of Israel (Revelation 7:4-8). I believe that these martyred saints of the tribulation period will receive their glorified bodies when the Lord comes to establish His kingdom. They will be a kind of "gleanings," completing the first resurrection (Revelation 20:4), which began with the raising of the dead saints of the church age and the translation of living believers at the rapture (1 Thessalonians 4:14). When Christ returns at the close of the tribulation, the entire company of raptured saints will very likely be part of the armies from Heaven that will follow Him "upon white horses, clothed in fine linen, white and clean" (Revelation 19:14). If an evaluation of the works of the martyred saints is necessary, we are not told when it will occur.

153. Revelation 7 refers to a body of believers as the 144,000, but in chapter 14 another group of the same number is mentioned. Who are the ones in the second reference?

I see no reason to believe that the 144,000 of Revelation 14 is a different company from those described earlier. You read in chapter 7 that these had been "sealed the servants of our God in their foreheads" (v. 3). In chapter 14, they are spoken of as "having His Father's name written in their foreheads" (v. 1). I conclude, therefore, that they are sealed and set apart for special ministry at the beginning of the tribulation. They are probably the heralds of the gospel of the kingdom, resulting in the conversion of the great multitude of Gentiles during that 7-year period. In chapter 14, this same number—144,000 out of the tribes of Israel—is seen again. This time it is at the close of the tribulation, when Jesus their Messiah stands upon the Mount of Olives as predicted in Zechariah 14:4.

TWENTY-FOUR ELDERS

154. Who are the 24 elders mentioned in the book of Revelation?

Most evangelical Bible students believe that the 24 elders are representative of the church in her reign with Christ. This is assumed because they sit upon thrones, are clothed in white raiment, and have crowns of gold. In addition, they have golden bowls filled with incense, which "are the prayers of saints" (Revelation 5:8). The crowns and bowls seem to indicate that they are both kings and priests. In Revelation 1:6 we read that Christ has "made us a kingdom of priests unto God."

However, some questions must be raised about this

interpretation. First, these elders always appear together, and they are quite distinct from the saints whose prayers they present to God. In their song in Revelation 5, for example, the elders make a distinction between themselves and the redeemed (most authorities agree that the pronouns "us" and "we" should be "them" and "they"): "Thou are worthy to take the scroll, and to open its seals; for Thou was slain, and hast redeemed [them] to God by Thy blood out of every kindred, and tongue, and people, and nation; and hast made [them] unto our God a kingdom of priests, and [they] shall reign on the earth" (Revelation 5:9,10).

Second, these elders are not symbolic, but definite individuals. In both Revelation 5:5 and 7:13 we are told that one of the 24 elders spoke with John.

Third, the church is the bride of Christ. But the bride will not be enthroned before her marriage with the Lamb, nor before her Bridegroom has taken His throne. Yet the 24 elders are enthroned before the marriage of the Lamb and before Christ is seated on His own throne.

Though I am not dogmatic on this, I believe the 24 elders are heavenly beings. They will no doubt serve as rulers, for they are called "elders" and are seated upon thrones. Their function will be that of government. Remember, in the heavenlies there are "authorities" and "principalities." In Daniel's account of his vision of Heaven, he said, "I beheld till the *thrones* were placed, and the Ancient of days did sit..." (Daniel 7:9). Note that there was not just one *throne* for the Ancient of days, but *thrones*. These 24 elders, therefore, were possibly vice-regents over the universe, appointed by God.

Daniel 10:13 speaks of "Michael, one of the chief priests...." This indicates that other princes were in God's council of heavenly creatures, having been placed by Him in positions of authority. It could be that the 24 elders make up this group of rulers under God, exercising responsibility in the government of the universe.

TWO IMMUTABLE THINGS

155. What are the two immutable things mentioned in Hebrews 6:18?

The context shows that this refers to the Old Testament example of Abraham, the father of the faithful (Galatians 3:26-29). God had declared that He would bless him, make of him a great nation, and give the land of Palestine to him and his seed after him. This promise was made before Isaac was born (read Genesis 12:1-3,7). This is the first of the two immutable things: the *promise* of God, His *Word*. After Isaac was born, God put the faith of Abraham to the test by demanding that he offer his son as a sacrifice. Abraham "believed God," and in so doing he gave up Isaac unto death (see Hebrews 11:17-19). He received him back "in a figure" by resurrection, for by the substitute ram, Isaac was given new life.

God then responded with the second of these two immutable things (Genesis 22:15-18). He said, "By Myself have I sworn." This was *God's oath*. The *promises* God had made concerning Israel and the Messiah were confirmed by *His oath*. These are the "two immutable things in which it was impossible for God to lie" — His Word, confirmed by His oath.

TWO WITNESSES

156. In Revelation 10:11, to whom must John prophesy? When and where? Could he be one of the two witnesses?

The revision of this verse in the *American Standard Version* renders it, "Thou must prophesy again *over* (or *concerning*) many peoples...." This is exactly what John proceeded to do in the following chapters. So his prophecy is not "before" many peoples, but rather "concerning" them. We may *not* assume from this that John is one of the two witnesses of chapter 11. Malachi 4:5, when compared with Christ's words in Matthew 17:11, seems to indicate that Elijah is one of the witnesses. I do not know who the second may be, and the Word of God is silent on this subject.

URIM AND THUMMIM

157. Please explain the use of the Urim and Thummim as found in Exodus 28:30.

And thou shalt put in the breastplate of judgment the Urim and the Thummim; and they shall be upon Aaron's heart, when he goeth in before the Lord: and Aaron shall bear the judgment of the children of Israel upon his heart before the Lord continually (Exodus 28:30).

The words "Urim" and "Thummim" mean literally "lights" and "perfections." The objects they refer to, however, are not specifically described in the Bible. We do know they were placed in the breastplate of the high priest, called the "breastplate of judgment" (or decision) in Exodus 28:30.

There is some indication that they were identified with the stones of the breastplate, and that they were used in various ways. We're told, for example, that Joshua stood before Eleazar to ask direction of "the judgment of Urim" (Numbers 27:21), and when Saul inquired of the Lord, it is recorded that "the Lord answered him not . . .by Urim" (1 Samuel 28:6). In some unique way, therefore, the Urim and Thummim were used by the high priest to determine the will of God.

WORKS

158. Please explain James 2:24 as compared to Galatians 2:16. James makes it sound as if works are necessary for justification. Is he speaking of salvation in this passage?

Ye see, then, that by works a man is justified, and not by faith only (James 2:24).

> Knowing that a man is not justified by the works
> of the law, but by the faith of Jesus Christ, even we
> have believed in Jesus Christ, that we might be
> justified by the faith of Christ, and not by the works of
> the law; for by the works of the law shall no flesh be
> justified (Galatians 2:16).

No, the James passage is not speaking of salvation. These two verses of Scripture are not contradictory. In Galatians, Paul's teaching shows that a man cannot be justified *before God* by the works of the law. James' words, however, are concerned with the believer's justification *before men*. In the context of his epistle, "works" means the believer's service and fruitfulness. As used by Paul, "works" are those deeds by which man tries to make himself acceptable to God. A Christian shows the reality of his faith in the Lord Jesus by his actions and testimony. Paul was speaking of positional justification declared by God, while James had in mind the visible evidence of that transforming grace (compare Ephesians 2:8,9 with Philippians 2:12,13).

SCRIPTURE INDEX

BOOK	QUESTION	BOOK	QUESTION
6:9-13	105,106	**Luke**	
6:14,15	141	1:5	85
6:27	8	1:17	44,45
7:6	79	3:4	44
7:21-23	127	3:17	5
8:11,12	66	3:38	54
8:22	27	5:37	99
10:5,6	66	9:23	28
10:10	66	9:59,60	27
10:37	27	10:18	109,133
12:34,36	63	11:29-32	73
12:40	73	13:3,5	114
13:41	83	15:4,6	99
16:18	41	Chapter 16	40,99
17:10-13	45,156	16:1-13	89
18:15-20	103	16:24	99
19:3-6	101	18:8	37
19:27	121	19:11-26	97
20:16	121	20:35,36	58
21:28-31	114	21:24	149
22:1-14	83	22:19	93
23:38	66	23:31	69
Chapter 24	47,96,137	24:25-47	114
24:13,14	47	24:36-43	14
24:22	48,151	24:50	57
24:35	46		
24:29,30	96	**John**	
24:29-40	82	1:12,13	54,107
24:48	83	1:18	52
Chapter 25	47	1:33	5
25:8-12	83	3:13	17
25:1-13	96	3:15,16	7,99
25:30	83	3:35	21
25:46	99	4:20	56,72
26:26-29	93,108	5:24	80
27:3-10	74	5:29	119
27:46	20	6:27	99
27:52,53	115	6:37	107
		6:39,44,54	84
		6:44	107
Mark		6:53-58	93
4:25	97	6:63	93
9:38-41	78	6:70,71	75
9:46-49	5	7:39	62
10:16	129	10:16	138
16:16	7	10:28,29	142

BOOK	QUESTION	BOOK	QUESTION
12:31	109	6:3-7	3
12:37-41	52,67	6:11	145
12:40	67	6:13	26
12:47,48	80	6:23	125
14:16	61	Chapter 7	36
14:17	125	7:13	36
15:7	102	8:1	77
16:12-15	112	8:11	116
16:24	106	8:16	146
Chapter 17	107	8:26,27	104
17:2,9,11	107	Chapters 9,	
17:12	10,75	10,11	66
17:26	91	10:9,10	7,63
18:36	81	10:17	1
20:17	19	10:20,21	66
		11:20	66
Acts		11:25	67,149
1:5	5	11:26,27	149
1:18,19	74	12:1	26
2:3	5	14:4,10-12	78
2:23	75	14:5	120
Chapter 5	142	16:20	135
6:1-7	56		
8:17	56	**1 Corinthians**	
Chapter 10	38	2:11-15	146
10:48	92	3:3	111
11:14	38	3:15	50,142
11:18	114	4:15	110
11:26	130	6:13	100
13:1-4	56	6:15-19	77
13:46	79	7:8	98
15:5	33	7:14	30
15:14	149	Chapter 9	88
15:23-25	33	9:20,22	33
16:1-3	33	9:24-27	50,122
16:16,17	8,42	10:11	12
16:31	7	10:13	105
17:29,30	114	11:23-26	92,93,95
19:1-7	6,56,92	11:27-29	94
22:16	8	12:10	147
26:10	98	12:11	56
		12:13	5
Romans		13:12	58
1:5	37	Chapter 15	39
2:4	114	15:12	4
4:3,5	130	15:19,20,29	4

BOOK	QUESTION	BOOK	QUESTION
15:44,49	39,58,117	**Philippians**	
15:51,52	111,112,-137	1:1	125
16:1,2	88	1:6	60
		2:9	21
2 Corinthians		2:12,13	125,158
4:4	109	3:9	83
4:10	77	3:11	118
5:1	117	3:21	100
5:8	117	4:15-19	88
5:1-10	76,77		
5:16	21	**Colossians**	
5:17	54,144	1:15	22
5:21	24,129	2:9	53
9:9	88		
11:14	42	**1 Thessalonians**	
12:1-5	133	1:9,10	114
12:14,15	110	3:13	124
13:5	77	Chapters 4,5	111,137
		4:13-18	76,152
Galatians		4:15-17	76,111,112,119
2:11	78	5:23	146
2:16	158		
2:20	28	**2 Thessalonians**	
3:11	49	1:8	5
3:26-29	155	2:2	111
5:4	49	2:3	10
5:19-21	29	2:7,8	60,113
6:1	103	2:9-12	131
6:6	88	3:6	78
6:14	28	3:14	78
Ephesians		**1 Timothy**	
1:4	151	1:12	8
1:7	77	2:8	57
2:2	109,133	2:9	35,57
2:6	21	4:1-3	84
2:8,9	7,49,125,-158	4:13,16	126
2:10	54	4:14	56
3:1-6	138		
4:9,10	40	**2 Timothy**	
4:30	61	1:6	56
4:32	141	2:25	114
5:21-33	101	3:1-8	2,84
6:18	104		

BOOK	QUESTION	BOOK	QUESTION
Titus		1:8	144,145
2:12	125	1:9	59,143,144.
3:5	125		145
		1:10	144,145
Hebrews		2:1,2	32,144
1:2	84	2:19	2
4:12	146	3:6,9	144
5:12-14	50	3:22	102
6:1-12	50	4:1	147
6:18	155	4:12	52
7:26	24	5:16	142
8:6-13	108	5:16,17	50,143
9:11,12	18		
9:26	77	**Jude**	
10:4	130	3	37
10:6,8	86	6,7	54
10:12	21	17-19	84
10:14	32		
10:19	142	**Revelation**	
10:26-30	142	1:6	154
10:37	60	1:7	64
11:4	1	2:17	91
11:10	65	3:12	91
11:17-19	155	Chapter 5	154
12:6	132	5:5	154
		5:8-10	154
James		Chapter 7	152,153
1:13,14	25,105,132	7:3	153
2:24	158	7:4-8	151
		7:4-17	152
1 Peter		7:9	131
1:2	107	7:13	154
1:19	24	7:14	59
2:24	24,77,129	9:18	48
3:1-3	35	10:11	156
3:18-21	23	Chapter 11	44,137,156
4:3	31	Chapter 12	133,135
4:6	31	12:9	109
		12:7-12	109,133
2 Peter		12:10	109
2:20-22	79,128	13:4	11
3:1-9	84	13:12	11
3:10	46,48	13:15	11
		Chapter 14	153
1 John		14:1	153
1:5	20		

126

BOOK	QUESTION
Chapter 17	9
17:1,15,16	9
17:8	10
19:6-9	76,77
19:11-16	76,152
Chapter 20	40
20:3-5	119,152
20:9	124
20:10	99
20:11	46
20:12,14	15,119
21:1	46
21:12	65
21:15-17	71
21:23	71
21:24	70
22:14	59

SUBJECT INDEX